HOLIER than THOU

Amazing Saint Stories You Have to Read to Believe

Mark Hart with Greg Iwinski

Cover design by David Calavitta.
Copy editing by Natalie Alemán and Danielle Rzepka.

ISBN: 978-0-9802362-2-4

Copyright ©2011 Life Teen, Inc. All rights reserved.

Published by Life Teen, Inc.
2222 S. Dobson Rd.
Suite 601
Mesa, AZ 85202
www.lifeteen.com

Printed in the United States of America.
Printed on acid-free paper.

For more information about Life Teen or to order additional copies, go online to www.lifeteen.com or call us at 1-800-809-3902.

·

Dedication

To all those souls who -
because of their love of God today -
will be known as Saints tomorrow...

Table of Contents

PREFACE

The saints are amazing; so it should come as no surprise to us that many of the occurrences within their lives are, likewise, amazing. So many of their stories are so extraordinary, in fact, that I felt the need to share some of my favorites in one place.

These are not the only miraculous stories of the saints by any means. There are innumerable stories not shared here that would make your jaws drop in shock and your knees bend in joyful reverence at the power and glory of God. My prayer is that this little book will serve as an appetizer for your spiritual reading; something to whet your intellectual appetite in the hope that you'll dive even more deeply into the lives and legacies of the heroic men and women who have come before us and offered their all to Christ.

The danger in reading a book like this is that it could put your mind and heart at odds with each other. You might find your heart leaping at the thought of God doing such amazing things through ordinary men and women while your mind is left doubting or wondering if such things could ever happen. Both responses are okay; in fact, they're good. It's in that tug-of-war between hope and "logic" that you can invite the Holy Spirit to breathe. It's on this battleground between head and heart that your faith will grow deeper and your hope stronger in the love of the Lord.

Faith does not contradict reason; faith exceeds reason.

If something in these brief biographies seems a little "too

hard to believe," first ask yourself this question, "Is it hard to believe because God *couldn't* do it or because God *wouldn't* do it?"

If we say God couldn't do it, then our view of God is too limited and we're trying to confine the Creator to the laws of creation. God is bigger than our imaginations, our limitations, and our sin. The God who created lightning, the giraffe, and chili peppers does not suffer from a lack of creativity.

If we say God wouldn't do it, we need to ask ourselves if God has ever acted in ways that seem to contradict our human "reason." This is the same God Who created everything from nothing, Who called upon murderers (Moses and Saul) to lead His people, and Who took on flesh through a virgin birth ... rarely does He do things "our way."

We cannot forget what God told us through the prophet Isaiah:

> *"For my thoughts are not your thoughts, neither are your ways my ways, says the Lord. For as the heavens are higher than the earth, so are my ways higher than your ways and my thoughts than your thoughts." – Isaiah 55:8-9*

So, *could* all of the miracles and incidents talked about in this book literally happen to and through these heroically holy men and women of the faith? Absolutely, yes.

Did all of these miracles and incidents take place exactly as described or as tradition and legend have retold them? Many of them (possibly all of them), yes. This side of heaven, we'll never know for sure.

Perhaps the more challenging question is whether or not you think these types of things could ever happen to or through *you*. Most of us don't think of ourselves as potential saints – not because we believe God is too small but because we believe ourselves to be too sinful.

The two things every saint in this book have in common is that they were all sinners and that they all believed that God's grace was bigger than their individual sin. Do you?

God desires to make you a saint, too. All you need to do is let Him.

INTRODUCTION

Have you ever heard of Saint Billy of Des Moines or Saint Nikki of Long Island?

Probably not, since they're not canonized, or "known," saints of the Church...yet.

Did you know that you are called to become a saint? That's right, God's call for you – before husband or priest or wife or sister or doctor or engineer or lion tamer (that'd be cool) – is to become a saint. Declining Christ's invitation to sainthood is life's greatest daily tragedy.

"Me, a *saint*?!? Um, no," you might think to yourself. "That's for *really* holy people."

You're created and designed to become a saint; whether or not the Catholic Church ever *canonizes* you as a saint is a whole different thing. That God wants you to live for Him, point others to Him, and be with Him forever in heaven is a fact.

Many times, Catholics (young and old) will question why the saints are important or how they are still relevant in modern times. The saints are our older brothers and sisters in the faith. We can always learn from them, even long after their earthly deaths. We are Christ's disciples, His students, and we can never lose our desire to learn more about Him or how to love Him more fully.

Our family is a foundational source of learning for us. Our family aids in the formation of our character. As Catholics, we have a rich family history from which to draw, a long lineage of heroic figures capable of guiding us to deeper and deeper levels of holiness and sanctity. The saints' example and their prayerful intercession for us are both gifts from God.

So, you might be asking yourself, *what is a saint, exactly?*

The word *saint* comes from the Latin word "sanctus," which means holy or set apart. Saint Paul first said it (Philippians 4:21) to mean *all* of the faithful early Christians. Our Church teaches that the saints occupy a hallowed (holy and special) place in heaven. That place is in the presence of what's called "the Beatific Vision" – it's basically front row center in God's heavenly throne room.

The Church doesn't say that every saint is named – far from it, actually. The ones we officially call "saints" are joined by countless others who lived "saintly" lives but haven't officially been investigated or titled saints by the Church. By best estimates, there are over 10,000 saints who are currently named – again, most saints are not named on earth but are known in heaven.

In fact, there are living, breathing saints around you right now, and not just the "Blessed Mother Teresa of Calcutta"-types that you see on television. There are saints in your own parish and neighborhood, very likely. Most of them will never enjoy the "title" on earth; but that's okay, since truly saintly people would never want the title anyway.

That being said, turn the page and read about your older brothers and sisters in the faith who have victoriously attained sainthood. They are proof that you can love God and still have exciting lives of passion, joy, and adventure.

Your story is still being written. Love God with everything you are and – who knows? – maybe one day someone will be reading about your life on the pages of a book just like this.

AMAZING SAINT STORIES YOU HAVE TO READ TO BELIEVE

Saint Agatha

Feast day: February 5th

Invoked against: the eruption of volcanoes, lightning, and fires

Modern science has done a great deal to combat and even conquer disease. There are some diseases, though, that continue to baffle and elude modern medicine as doctors and researchers scramble to find a cure. One of the most devastating modern battles is the war against breast cancer, with millions of women fighting it and millions of families prayerfully uniting in hope of a cure. One of the greatest weapons in this battle may be none other than an obscure Catholic saint from the early Church.

Not much is known about Agatha, historically speaking. We know that she was born in Sicily in the early to mid third century and was martyred during the reign of Emperor Decius around A.D. 251. Agatha was apparently raised in a wealthy and powerful family. At a young age she dedicated herself (and, thus, her virginity) to God. Ancient texts speak of her remarkable beauty as well.

A high-ranking Senator named Quintianus was quite taken by her, but Agatha, dedicated to God and seeking only His love, spurned Quintianus' advances and proposals of marriage. Enraged, Quintianus had her imprisoned in a brothel in an attempt to break her of her stubbornness. After a month of humiliation and assault, Agatha returned without ever breaking her vow. Quintianus, even more aggravated, then sent Agatha to prison, where she was tortured. At one point, according to legendary accounts, he even had her breasts cut off in the cruelest act of abuse. At this time,

Saint Peter reportedly appeared to her in prison and, by the grace of God, healed her. All were amazed at her miraculous healing.

Over time, however, the assaults and beatings became more than her mortal body could bear and she was martyred for the faith, still a virgin and very in love with the Lord.

It is for this reason that Agatha is invoked as the patroness against breast disease and is such an intercessory ally not only in the fight against breast cancer but also against rape, abuse, all forms of mistreatment of women, and against assaults on human dignity.

Some say that the stories of her imprisonments, torture, and healing are simply legend – mere folklore used to inspire people but lacking in historical accuracy, and that "all we know for sure" is that she lived and died a martyr's death.

Perhaps.

Many in the early church, however, strongly venerated (honored and respected) her life and memory, rejoicing in her heroism and asking for her prayers. Her life has inspired people in need of hope for hundreds of years.

Breast cancer is a common enemy, one that has the ability to unite people of faith and souls who have yet to encounter or accept the love and the mercy of God. It's in situations like these that Catholics have a great opportunity to reach out in love, both to the family around them (on earth) and the family that came before them (in heaven).

This culture needs all the help it can get to change its perspective – to better honor and protect women and to uphold the dignity of life within a culture of death. So ask Saint Agatha, true model of virtue, to pray with you; not only for a cure for cancer, but also for a change of heart and for greater reverence for both the dignity of the human person and the gift of our bodies, which are temples of the Holy Spirit (1 Corinthians 6:19).

Saint Agnes

Feast day: January 21st

Patron of: bodily purity, chastity, engaged couples, gardeners, Girl Scouts, girls, rape victims, and virgins

We are warned in Scripture to beware of "wolves in sheep's clothing" (Matthew 7:15). When speaking about Saint Agnes, however, someone should have warned the pagans of the time that this little beauty was like a lion in sheep's clothing: brave, bold, and beautiful. Saint Agnes was not a young Catholic you'd want to mess with.

Back in 304 AD – when Christianity was still illegal – a variety of young suitors came to thirteen-year-old Agnes wanting to marry her. One of them, Eutropius, was even the son of the governor. Agnes replied that Christ was to be her only spouse, her only love. Angered by the response, the governor himself offered Agnes lavish gifts, riches, and a title of honor if she would change her mind and marry his pagan son. Agnes again refused. He then displayed a variety of ancient torture devices, threatening her in an effort to change her mind. Agnes replied, "You will soon learn that my God is a God of purity. He will bring your wicked purpose to naught." One has to think that, at this point, God was just smiling down on His beautiful young daughter.

The governor, on the other hand, was not smiling. Agnes was dragged before the statue of a false goddess and told to worship. She promptly refused and, instead, lifted her arms and prayed aloud to her God, Jesus Christ. They tried putting handcuffs on her, which only slipped off. She was then beaten, tortured, and stripped naked. She was to be led through the city streets for all to see and to mock and later placed in a brothel and treated as a prostitute.

At the moment Agnes' clothes were removed, however, legend has it that her hair miraculously grew long enough to conceal her nakedness and protect her from shame. Those are some lavish locks! (It's at this point that we pause to tell the Brothers Grimm that they may owe some royalty reparations to the Church. Can anyone say "Rapunzel"?)

They threw Agnes in the brothel, regardless. No sooner did the door shut than an angel appeared with a stunning white garment for her to wear. No "customers" dared talk to her, except one: her former suitor, Eutropius. His lewd comments not only exposed his true depravity but also left him blind (or dead, depending upon which accounts you believe). Agnes did not rejoice; instead, she prayed over him, and he was cured. Following that little miracle, she was charged with witchcraft and was sentenced to die. She was beheaded not long after and died both a virgin and a martyr.

Agnes still has a huge following over 1700 years later. This bold teenage girl serves as an example of purity for young Catholic women of every culture. Some traditions encourage young women to dream of their future spouses on the eve of Agnes' feast day (January 21st) and to fast the entire day as a form of faithfulness and prayer. You'll often see icons of Agnes holding a lamb, her symbol, because Agnes sounds a lot like *agnus*, which is Latin for "lamb."

Saint Agnes reminds us that purity seeks purity and sin seeks sin. Whenever you are struggling with temptation, fearful of mockery for your faith, or scared to stand for Christ, invite Saint Agnes to pray for you; God's grace will unleash the lion inside of His lamb.

Saint Alphonsus de Liguori

Feast day: August 1st

Patron of: confessors, moralists, theologians, final perseverance, and vocations

Invoked against: arthritis and scrupulosity

Picture the smartest person in your high school. Picture the Valedictorian – the kid who finishes the SAT in record time, who never studies yet gets straight A's without ever breaking a sweat. Odds are, Saint Alphonsus was smarter. Many considered Alphonsus to be a child prodigy. This is a guy who earned his doctorate in law from the University of Naples (Italy) at sixteen years old. Yes, you read that correctly; while modern sixteen-year-olds are worried about passing their driving test, Alphonsus was finishing his Ph.D. By the age of twenty-one he wasn't out bar-hopping; he'd opened his own legal practice, and it's said that he never once attended court if he hadn't first attended Mass. Put simply (for those of us who were not Valedictorian), Saint Alphonsus Liguori was one really smart and very holy dude.

In about 1725, he was ordained a priest and soon after founded the Congregation of the Most Holy Redeemer, a religious order known as the Redemptorists (which is still around today). He was a skilled writer with a brilliant legal mind and was known as an expert in moral theology. In 1762, Pope Clement XIII named him a bishop. Even with all of these accomplishments, however, many knew of him because of the miraculous reports that constantly surrounded his daily life.

Alphonsus was a visionary and capable of bilocating. It's said that he would be hearing confessions (which he did for hours each day) in one city and simultaneously preaching in another. It was reported, too, that he sat for an entire day in a chair in Naples – an account verified by multiple witnesses – while also sitting at the bedside of Pope Clement XIV while he died. He was seen levitating on more than one occasion, and several members of his order said that Alphonsus would often read his book of prayers in the chapel all night long – which might not seem that miraculous...wait for it ... if it weren't for the fact that he read the book *by the light of his own face*. Again, the answer is, "Yes, you read that correctly." Alphonsus was so holy that his countenance provided all the reading light he needed in the dimly lit chapel. Jesus, "the light of the world" (John 8:12), told us to "let our light shine before men" (Matthew 5:16), but few saints have ever taken Christ's call so literally.

Although he was in poor health for a good portion of his life, Alphonsus worked tirelessly to reform clergy, preach and teach the truth of the Christ's Church, and reignite the fire of faith in a time when the Church badly needed revitalization.

It's said that Saint Alphonsus died a peaceful death and went home to heaven at ninety years old. He is still respected as one of the finest minds in the Communion of Saints and he is one of only twenty-six saints to be declared a Doctor of the Church.

If you're praying about your life and future and seeking God's wisdom on how you can best put your gifts and talents to work for the Kingdom, ask Saint Alphonsus to pray with you. God has a plan to use every talent you've been given for His glory, if you let Him.

Saint Ambrose

Feast day: December 7th

Patron of: bee keepers, bees, candle makers, domestic animals, learning, students, wax refiners, and school children.

They say politics and religion don't mix, but Saint Ambrose of Milan had a life that led him right from one into the other – and (thankfully) not in a way that led to heresy. In fact, this "sweet-tongued saint" (stay tuned to find out why we call him that) turned out to be a great defender of truth against the heresy of Arianism.

Ambrose was the son of a Roman senator, and as a young man he became the governor of Milan. He was a good governor, but that was pretty much it – the guy wasn't even baptized, let alone a saint. The job of governor was fine until the Bishop of Milan died; then things got sticky. See, the Arian heresy (it's the one that says Jesus wasn't divine) was rampant in Milan in the fourth century. The Bishop of Milan himself was actually a believer in Arianism – obviously "no bueno" (or is that "no buono" if it's in Milan?) for the "upholding the truth in the Church" department.

Either way, the Bishop's death caused a large uproar in the city as the faithful members of the Church argued with the heretics about who the next bishop should be. Ambrose, being an upstanding governor, headed into the fray. His pleas for peace and civility so won over the crowds that they demanded that Ambrose be their new bishop.

Well, good old Ambrose knew that a life as a bishop would be far more dangerous than being a governor would be, so he did the ol' "Jonah shuffle" and ran away from his calling

(Jonah 1:3). When people finally tracked him down, he told them he wasn't even a baptized Catholic and that there was no way he could be a bishop. His protests fell on deaf ears, and he was baptized and ordained all at the same time – talk about a two-for-one!

Now, the story could turn out like any other at this point. Ambrose could have lived like a politician and priest, following in the footsteps of some bad examples in Church history. Instead, he completely embraced the life of the Church, sold all that he had and devoted himself to the study of theology and philosophy. He became the Arians' worst nightmare: a passionate, eloquent bishop who was determined to stamp out heresy.

If you find yourself under attack for your faith, Saint Ambrose is a great intercessor to have in your corner. When you stand for truth, not only do you defend the faith, but you will also help others to abandon the world's lies in favor of the freedom only found in Jesus Christ. Ambrose brought many souls to Christ, and he baptized one person you'll probably recognize: a certain guy by the name of Augustine. Wherever he went, Ambrose preached the truth – something it seems he had been born to do. When he was a baby, the story goes, a swarm of bees came out of the sky and started crawling around his mouth. None of the bees stung infant Ambrose; instead, they left honey on his lips – a foreshadowing of what his words would be like later in life. Now all can agree that's a pretty *sweet* story.

Saint Anthony of Padua

Feast day: June 13th

Patron of: American Indians, amputees, animals, elderly people, expectant mothers, poor people, pregnant women, sailors, seekers of lost articles, starving people

Invoked against: barrenness, shipwreck, starvation, and sterility

If you want a confirmation name that strikes fear into the hearts of evildoers, you might want to go with Anthony of Padua. His nickname alone makes you think of pro-wrestling: "The Hammer of Heretics." If you need a tag-team partner in heaven, this is the saint for you.

Anthony was loved and revered, even in his own time, and was canonized a saint less than a year after his death. He grew up as an Augustinian, but at the age of twenty-six had an experience that drew him to the Franciscans. When the bodies of the first Franciscan martyrs – five of them – were brought to the monastery where Anthony lived, he knew he wanted to be Franciscan. He desired martyrdom so much that he began to follow in their footsteps – talk about being hardcore Catholic!

Like any good hero, Anthony didn't just walk the walk; he could talk the talk, too. The Franciscan leaders decided young Anthony would preach. When he began to speak about Scripture, everyone was amazed at the powerful beauty of his words.

Legends spread quickly, even in the 1200s, and soon huge crowds came to hear Anthony speak. Once, when he was preaching, the crowd was too big to fit into the Church, so the young Franciscan went outside to tell them the truth of the Gospel. While he was speaking, a huge storm rolled into town – but nothing could stop the voice of Anthony; no one in the crowd felt a single drop of rain, even though the storm raged all around them.

Anthony loved preaching, so much so that one Holy Thursday, in the middle of a sermon, he realized he was supposed to be leading a song for his brothers at night prayer. If you've ever needed to be in two places at once, you'll love this miracle: Anthony paused his preaching, instantly appeared with his brothers to sing at night prayer, and then he resumed his preaching.

No heretic was safe from Anthony's preaching; his zeal for the truth was endless, and his explanation of the faith was so simple that even those who couldn't read or write could understand. He *had* to preach and glorify God all the time, and when a group of heretics refused to listen to him, he went to a local lake and preached to the fish. A huge school of fish gathered and stood on their tail fins to hear the saint speak, and soon a crowd of people came to see what was going on. One could say that whenever Anthony spoke, "school" was in session.

The young man with the powerful voice for God was often ill, and at the age of 36 he died of dropsy. When he died, children wept in the streets and church bells rang without anyone ringing them. And that isn't even the end of his legacy. When his body was examined later, everything had decomposed – that is, everything except his tongue, still not decomposed and as pure as the words that came from it.

Now, at this point in the story you might be wondering why people pray to Anthony to help them find lost things (if you weren't wondering that, it'd be a good time to wonder it now). Once when Anthony was younger he had a book of psalms – that was quite valuable to his daily prayer and teaching – stolen from him. When Anthony realized it was missing he immediately prayed that it be found or returned.

The prayer evidently worked; the thief's guilt grew so great that he not only returned the book but also repented and begged for forgiveness.

Saint Anthony lived boldly for God. Ask him to pray for you when you are called to bear witness to the truth, especially to people who might not be open to it. Feel free to throw up a prayer or two when you're missing something important, too. To this day, people still invoke Saint Anthony to help them find everything from car keys, to receipts, to sunglasses. And while you're at it, be sure to thank God that Saint Anthony doesn't charge for downloads!

Saint Barbara

Feast day: December 4th

Patron of: architects, bomb technicians, construction workers, dying people, firefighters, fireworks manufacturers, prisoners, sailors, and sudden death

Invoked against: lightening, death artillery, explosions, fire and storms

Remember a few pages back when Saint Agnes' hair miraculously grew to conceal her nakedness? Well, if the Brothers Grimm did steal any part of their Rapunzel story from Saint Agnes' biography, they must have also plundered some little factoids from the life of Saint Barbara.

So what kind of life, one might ask, would result in Barbara being known as the patroness of, among other things, lightning, fireworks makers, and sailors? The answer: an exciting life, to be sure.

Many teenage daughters are forced to deal with overprotective fathers, but (probably) few have it quite as bad as Barbara did. Her father, Dioscurus, was a very overbearing and jealous man. Barbara was a tremendous beauty, so much so that Dioscurus hid her away in a tower (cue the Rapunzel soundtrack) so that no young man could ever see her unmatched beauty. The story of Barbara's beauty and "incarceration" spread and, eventually, a young Christian disguised as a physician was allowed to visit an ailing Barbara in the tower. This Christian introduced Barbara to the Gospel and instructed her in the faith. Though Barbara was raised a pagan (believing in and following false gods), her large amounts of free time (because she didn't have

Facebook up in her tower) led to an openness to study religion. She quickly decided that paganism was illogical and empty and that Christianity was the faith of truth. The young damsel (in tower-induced distress) quickly fell in love with Love – Jesus Christ.

While Dioscurus was away on business, workers were constructing a large bathing pool near the tower. Soon after, the water from the pool was found to have the miraculous power to heal and cure sickness because of Barbara's holiness. During that time, Barbara asked the workers to add a third window in her tower to symbolize the Holy Trinity. Though reluctant, the workers obliged. Upon his return, seeing the third window, the pagan Dioscurus drew his sword, preparing to kill Barbara. Before the blade touched her neck, she leapt from the tower window and flew (yes, *flew*) away to the mountains, where she hid in a cave. When an evil shepherd found Barbara and disclosed her location to her father, the young saint cursed him – turning the shepherd to stone and his sheep to locusts. Apparently all that time in the tower left young Barbara with some anger management issues.

When Dioscurus found her, he dragged her by the hair before the courts. When ordered to renounce her faith, Barbara refused. She was stripped and flogged. Again, she would not deny her God. So Dioscurus did what any maniacal, insane, godless father would do: he carried his daughter up the side of a mountain where he cut off her head. At that moment, thunder clapped and lightning descended from the heavens, striking and consuming the father, leaving only a pile of ash. To this day, all who fear lightning and handle fireworks or other explosives ask for God's protection through Barbara's intercession. Sailors, too, invoke her prayers on their behalf when navigating dangerous stretches of coast like those found outside of ... wait for it ... *Santa Barbara.*

Saint Barbara's story is almost unbelievable, which is why, when the Church investigated it centuries later, they took her out of the calendar of saints. Although still venerated by people across the world, this tale of holiness may be just that – a tale. However, several miracles have been attributed to Barbara, especially for those who are about to die and desire the Sacraments. She is the patron of receiving Sacraments before death, after reportedly bringing the Eucharist to Saint Stanislaus Kostka in the 1500s ... but that's another story.

God sends people into our lives bearing truth when we need it, just as He did with the Christian who went to Barbara's tower. Our job, like Saint Barbara, is to be open enough to receive it, and then bold enough to live it out – no matter the consequence. God watches over His children. God never abandons us; He protects us with perfect power and justice (Isaiah 41:10-11). Saint Barbara reminds us that we are not called to live in fear while in this world, but to live in hope for the next. Oh, and no matter how early your curfew is, your father is probably a saint compared to hers.

Saint Benedict

Feast day: July 11th

Patron of: dying people, Europe, farm workers, monks, people in religious orders, and students

Invoke against: fever, gallstones, inflammatory diseases, kidney disease, poison, temptations, and witchcraft

The name "Benedict" comes from the Latin meaning "he who is blessed." After reading about his life, however, some might argue that his name should be *Indestructibilis*, from the Latin for "he who is indestructible."

You've probably heard of Saint Benedict before. One of the most famous saints, he began a religious order known as the Benedictines. The motto of the Benedictine order is *ora et labora*, meaning "pray and work," which is fitting because Benedict constantly did both.

Born in Italy around 480, he had a twin sister who is also a saint (Saint Scholastica), which makes for a pretty impressive family tree. Benedict was special, even at a young age. After performing his first miracle (repairing a dish that was accidentally broken), Benedict began worrying that his classmates were too unholy and unfocused. He left school and fled to the mountains, where he lived as a hermit for three years in a cave. The Lord provided food for him through either a fellow hermit or a raven. Yes, a raven ... his own private delivery bird. Kind of cool, huh?

Benedict was constantly under attack from the devil. At one point, the devil tormented Benedict by reminding him of a beautiful woman he'd once seen. In response, Benedict immediately took off his robes and thrust himself into a thorn bush. The fact that he rarely struggled with sexual temptation after that has left many parents and youth ministers contemplating the use of the "thorn bush approach" in chastity talks with teens.

He founded a monastery and wrote a "rule of life" – a set of guidelines that he and his fellow monks would live by – centered on the concept of *ora et labora* (the Benedictines still follow this rule today). Benedict was not a "do as I say, not as I do" kind of guy. He set the bar high...really high when it came to discipline. Some of his fellow monks thought his way of life was too much, and there was an attempt made on Benedict's life. First, they poisoned his drink; but before taking a sip, the saint said a blessing and the cup shattered. Later they tried poisoning Benedict's bread, only to have the miraculous raven swoop in, clutch the loaf, and carry it away. To paraphrase Edgar Allen Poe, "Quoth the raven ... don't mess with Benedict."

Not quite "feeling the love," Saint Benedict soon returned to his cave, where people came to him for guidance, formation, and counsel. As he got older he didn't slow down – he eventually formed another twelve monasteries according to his rule of life. It's said that Benedict could read not only minds but also souls. He had the gift of prophecy and could foresee spiritual attacks of the devil before they happened. He healed the sick. He raised the dead. It's even said that he made a fierce barbarian named Galea faint, just by looking at him.

When the monks could no longer handle descending the steep and treacherous terrain to retrieve water for their mountaintop monastery, they asked Benedict to pray. He did, and the next day a fountain sprang forth on top of the mountain. As Benedict traveled around, the power of God went with him. He fearlessly destroyed pagan statues and altars and battled demons face to face. He eventually died in 547 (a date that he prophesied, by the way) while praying and was buried in the same tomb as his saintly sister.

Saint Benedict and the countless Benedictines who have followed in his footsteps are tremendous reminders to us of the importance of both working hard and praying hard. Saint Benedict is a great example of how to pray; everything he did was a form of prayer. Look around at the activities within your day and find ways to offer them up to God. Working in the yard, doing homework, exercising, cleaning the house – all of these can be offered as prayers to God, to help you grow in holiness. And if you ever wonder if your friends are true friends, you might want to invest in a raven.

Saint Benedict the Black

Feast day: April 4th

Patron of: African missions and African-Americans

Lots of us have heard of *the* Saint Benedict – if not because of his medals, universities, and religious order, then because a certain Bishop of Rome took on his name a few years ago (take a second ... yes, *Pope* Benedict XVI). But there have been a few other famous Benedicts, including one who could put any Iron Chef to shame.

Benedict was the son of Christopher and Diana, two slaves taken from Africa to Sicily. When he turned eighteen, Benedict was freed but continued to work for his former master as an employee. A few years later, some other workers in the town began to make fun of Benedict for his dark skin, but he responded with his graceful and cheery personality. A hermit who was passing by heard the exchange and stuck up for Benedict – a move that impressed the future saint so much that he sold what he had and became a hermit as well. When Pope Pius IV disbanded the hermits and created communities, Benedict became a Franciscan. He quickly took the job of cook, and loved to practice generosity in the kitchen.

If *Hell's Kitchen* is in New York, Heaven's Kitchen was with Benedict. He would feed anyone who came in need of food, and no matter how much he gave away there would always be enough. (There's a guy in the Gospels who did that too.) Some of the brothers said that when he cooked, there were angels helping him – now that definitely gives "angel food cake" a whole new meaning, doesn't it?

Benedict's hard work and service meant that (against his will) he became a superior, and then a master of the order's novices. Even though he hadn't been properly taught to read, he would preach deep theological truths to students. Eventually, however, he was allowed to return to the job he loved – cooking food for those who needed it.

Food wasn't the only thing Benedict was good at – he was also an excellent confessor, and people would travel just to experience the Sacrament with him. His deep insights led some to say he could read hearts in the confessional, and his cheerful attitude never faded. In his moments of ecstasy in prayer, his face would actually glow with light (talk about having a bright personality!). Benedict died of an illness in 1589, on the very date he had predicted (prophesied).

If you ever feel like an outsider or are mocked for being a little "different," Saint Benedict the Black is a great saint to have praying beside you. A man of true humility, he lived to serve God in his fellow man. Ask the Lord to develop your heart of service like our brother Benedict had, and watch as God brings people into your life who are hungry ... for His love.

Saint Cassian of Imola

Feed Day: August 13th

Patron of: Mexico City, stenographers, and teachers

Ahh, the joys of school: breezy hallways, mandatory assemblies, and scents of questionably produced meats wafting through the air (and that's not even mentioning actual *class*). Days become weeks become months become semesters... sometimes it seems like it just goes on and on forever. Summer break is only so long, and on the other side lurks another nine months of sitting in class watching the clock. Okay, maybe your school day's not *entirely* like that, but even the best student has a subject or two they can't stand. There's always that one class, that *one* teacher, where sitting through the period is a little like torture, right?

Well, in some classrooms it's not the teacher that's the problem – it's the students. In the competition for "Worst Class Ever," Saint Cassian of Imola would win. Cassian lived in Italy in the fourth century, and he was a Christian doing his best to follow the Lord while he did his job as a schoolteacher. He shared the skills of reading and writing with his young pupils, even teaching them a form of shorthand (which has made him the patron saint of court stenographers – bet you didn't know they *had* a patron saint). And through it all, he proclaimed Christ in the midst of an empire that was persecuting His followers. Cassian's faith didn't sit well with a local judge – a judge who had the ear of the Roman emperor. Before long, Cassian found himself in a position familiar to many about-to-be saints: he was ordered to deny his faith and make a sacrifice to false pagan gods.

Surprise, surprise: Cassian refused to abandon his faith in God. Instead of a regular execution, the judge decided to sentence the teacher to a particularly slow and painful death – one that didn't use the regular torturers. Cassian was tied to a stake and slowly stabbed to death by...his own students. About 200 young boys used their iron styli (that's the plural of "stylus," the thing you use on a touchscreen) to martyr their teacher, all the while mocking him for the faith that had lead him to this death. The ancient writer Prudentius said that the saint was "bloodied with a thousand little wounds," eventually bleeding to death in the midst of the crowd of children. To be clear, that's *not* why they say the pen's mightier than the sword – but thankfully, God's grace is mightier than both.

Saint Cassian's short and not-too-sweet story is worthy of mention on multiple levels. Teachers have a difficult enough task trying to shape young minds without the added stress and pressure of doing it within a pagan society. In honoring Saint Cassian, we honor true teachers everywhere who refuse to bend their morals to what is popular or accepted within the ever-shifting sands of culture. Ask Saint Cassian to pray with you and intercede for those men and women who continue to "fight the good fight" and teach truth in schools and universities where taking such a heroic stand is neither praised or welcomed. Pray, too, that those in charge of education would be people of high morals, convicted and prayerful, ensuring that the young minds entrusted to their care would receive nothing less than the truth of God and a knowledge of His great love.

Saint Catherine of Alexandria

Feast day: November 25th

Patron of: apologists, educators, girls, lawyers, librarians, libraries, philosophers, potters, preachers, secretaries, teachers, and theologians

You know that one friend you have, the one who's always right whenever there's a debate? The one with the rather explosive personality who always seems to have the right answers? You may want to introduce them to the life of Saint Catherine of Alexandria, because she's probably praying for them.

Catherine was the daughter of nobility but, like some other princesses in this book, she decided she'd rather serve in God's kingdom than reign in man's. As a young girl, this saint-to-be told her family she'd only marry someone who was smarter, more beautiful, wealthier, and socially higher than herself. (Jesus, anyone?)

Before her baptism, Catherine had a dream that the Blessed Mother asked the infant Jesus to accept her into the Kingdom. Christ responded that she had not yet been baptized, and turned away His face. Catherine immediately sought the Sacrament (who wouldn't after a dream like that?) and was baptized. She then had the dream again, and this time Jesus put a beautiful ring on her finger...and when she woke up, the ring was still on her hand (beat that, all you guys with super-cool engagement stories).

She abandoned her pagan faith as a teen and became skilled in Catholic philosophy and debate. When the emperor began to persecute believers in Christ, Catherine went to talk to him, and her beauty and poise earned her an audience.

Girls, if you ever thought Catholicism was about being timid or dainty, Catherine's here to smash that notion into pieces. She was such a skilled speaker that the emperor couldn't refute any of her arguments against paganism. Frustrated, he brought in fifty pagan philosophers to prove her wrong. Once again, Catherine's faith and intelligence made room for a miracle – the philosophers realized the falsehoods of paganism and converted on the spot (woo hoo!). Then, the enraged emperor immediately martyred them (boo ... hoo?).

Catherine wasn't done with inspiring conversions. After this young philosopher was thrown in prison, the wife of the emperor and the head of his royal guard came to visit her. Both converted to the faith, along with two hundred of the royal guard – and all were martyred. But now the emperor was without a wife, so he tried one final offer to Catherine to marry him (you can probably see where this is going).

She said no, and was sentenced to die on what is now known as a "Catherine Wheel" – a set of wheels and sharp blades that would pull and cut a person apart. As she was brought before it, Catherine prayed and an angel destroyed the machine. Maybe destroyed isn't the right word; the machine exploded, spikes and blades flew everywhere, and some pagans who had come to see the bloodshed were actually killed by debris. Eventually, Catherine was beheaded; but instead of blood, milk flowed from her wounds as she died, which is an insanely cool miracle, even if you're lactose intolerant.

For those who believe in Christ, death is never the end – and it was just the beginning for Saint Catherine. She's traditionally known as one of the "Fourteen Most Helpful Saints in Heaven," although we don't know if that's an official ranking up in the Kingdom. She's even helped out other saints here on earth: when Saint Joan of Arc heard those voices in heaven, one of them was Saint Catherine of Alexandria (talk about some supernatural girl power). If you're looking for a bold saint, one who will inspire you to great and heroic work for the Kingdom, look no further than Saint Catherine of Alexandria. If we were all as courageous as she, the world would be a much holier place.

Saint Catherine of Bologna

Feast day: March 9th

Patron of: art, artists, liberal arts, and painters

Invoked against: temptations

The name Catherine means "pure." Maybe that's why so many holy women and great saints share the name. You've already read about Saint Catherine of Alexandria, and before we introduce you to Saint Catherine of Siena, we thought we would "sandwich" another Catherine in between: Saint Catherine of *Bologna* (oh, c'mon – you didn't expect to make it an entire page without a bologna joke, did you?).

This Catherine obviously made the devil nervous – so nervous that at a very young age she was tormented by attacks from the Evil One that began to make her doubt Christ's True Presence in the Eucharist. Her prayerfulness carried her through, however; this "doubter" went on to become a visionary, a prophetess, an exquisite painter, a mystic, an abbess (someone who runs an abbey of nuns), and even a miracle worker (so remember her the next time you feel like you're a "terrible person" for having doubts in your faith).

Being the daughter of a diplomat had its privileges, and Catherine was fortunate to serve as a handmaid to a nobleman's daughter – affording her the opportunity for an amazing education. At fourteen years old she became a Franciscan tertiary; later, she became a Poor Clare, and eventually established a Poor Clare convent in Bologna (which is in Italy, by the way) in the mid fifteenth century (1456, to be exact).

It's been said that on one Christmas Eve, Catherine of Bologna recited one thousand decades of the Rosary. (Who says you need to *buy* your Christmas gifts? Prayer never goes out of style.) Not only did the Blessed Mother, holding the baby Jesus, appear to her in a vision, but Our Lady even allowed Catherine to experience holding the Christ Child in her own arms. That's right – pray a thousand decades in a day and Mother Mary might even let you babysit the Lord!

Catherine apparently illustrated her breviary (book of prayers containing the Liturgy of the Hours) with such skill that she is the patroness of (among other things) artists and painters. She was also considered an expert on how to handle spiritual attacks. She wrote extensively (did we mention she was an author, too?) about how to arm yourself to battle evil. Here's one excerpt:

Whoever wishes to carry the cross for his sake must take up the proper weapons for the contest, especially those mentioned here. First, diligence; second, distrust of self; third, confidence in God; fourth, remembrance of Passion; fifth, mindfulness of one's own death; sixth, remembrance of God's glory; seventh, the injunctions of Sacred Scripture following the example of Jesus Christ in the desert.

While she died from natural causes, many supernatural things have happened since she went home to heaven. She was buried without any embalming and reportedly entombed without a coffin. A sweet odor began emanating from her burial spot – so sweet that the perfumed odor began to draw attention from a good distance away. Some time later, Catherine of Bologna was exhumed from her grave to reveal that her body was incorrupt. To this day, over 500 years later, you can see the incorrupt remains of Catherine. She is encased behind glass in the very convent (chapel) where she lived. On display with her is the breviary she illustrated – still in vibrant condition.

So, if you're ever looking for a multi-talented saint to intercede on your behalf when you're under spiritual attack, or if you're looking for some writings to satisfy your spiritual "hunger," stop by Bologna and check in on Saint Catherine.

Saint Catherine of Siena

Feast day: April 29th

Patron of: Europe, firefighters, nurses, sick people, and those ridiculed for their piety

Invoked against: illness, miscarriages, and sexual temptation

With the stories of some saints, we have little more to go on than a paragraph and a legend (we're looking at you, Saint Christopher). There are others, though, who have entire books written about their journeys following Christ – and some wrote the book themselves! One such saint is a four-teenth century woman who was ready to follow Christ's call no matter what, even if it meant giving the Pope some real estate advice.

They say Catholics have big families, and Catherine's family set the bar: she was one of the youngest of twenty-five children (and you thought the family rolling up to Mass in a twelve-passenger van was big). From an early age, Catherine showed extreme holiness. When she was only six years old, she would see visions of guardian angels protecting people throughout their day.

Catherine wanted to be a third-order Dominican (like Martin de Porres, who's also in this book), but her parents weren't keen on the idea. A plague called the Black Death was sweeping through Siena, and over half her siblings had died either in disease or at their births. Catherine's parents wanted her to get married, but she knew that she was des-tined for a life married to Christ. As a teenager, she cut her hair off and refused to eat until her father finally allowed her to join the Dominicans. (Teens reading this might want to reconsider this tactic – it worked for Saint Catherine, but it might make that prom picture less than ideal.)

Her life was an interesting mix of joy and sorrow; although she suffered persecution and physical illness, during prayer she experienced amazing graces. Once, when she could not go to Communion, she prayed that God would make a way for her to receive. An angel took a piece of the host from the altar and brought it to Catherine. In some of her visions, she even received the Eucharist from Christ himself. And, like Saint Catherine of Alexandria (who's in another part of this book), this Catherine also experienced a spiritual marriage to Christ.

But a life of only internal prayer was far from all God had in store for Catherine. After a powerful vision of heaven, hell, and Purgatory, the Lord told Catherine to go out into the world – and she did. Traveling through Italy, this future saint (who was now only in her twenties) took on corruption and hypocrisy throughout the Church; she was bold in her proclamation to laity and to priests that only by complete love of Christ could the world be changed.

Catherine was "just" a young woman in the eyes of society, but her boldness to speak the truth lead her all the way to Avignon, France, where Pope Gregory XI was living. Because of schisms and politics (and above all, sin) the papacy had left Rome. Catherine implored the Pope to return to Rome and to reform the clergy of the Church. He did both, and she became one of his closest advisors.

This amazing young woman, who saw guardian angels and made Popes relocate, died at the age of thirty-three, while fighting to heal the Great Schism that sprung up during her final years. Before she was called to heaven, she dictated *The Dialogue*, a piece of theological writing so profound that she is now known as one of the Doctors of the Church.

Saint Catherine was feared by some and misunderstood by many because of her faith; her own family didn't know what to do with her. If you ever feel like people just don't quite "get" you because of your love for God or how you live out your faith, ask Saint Catherine to pray with you. Her example raises the bar for all of us to live a life of abandonment to God, even if it strains some of our earthly relationships. She put God first and, as a result, she didn't just change "her world" but also *the* world, as we know it today.

Saint Charbel

Feast day: December 24th

Patron of: Lebanon and the Middle East

Invoked against: paralysis

What comes to mind when you hear the term "roughing it"? Do you envision a camping trip without electricity? Perhaps you think of a hotel room without room service or wireless Internet? Maybe your idea of roughing it means that there's no charge left on your cell phone or, worse yet, you forgot your cell at home and had to go the entire day without the eternal blessing of text messaging. Whatever the case, odds are that your life looks very little like that of an obscure Lebanese monk now known as Saint Charbel.

Youseff was born in 1828 in a small, mountain village in Lebanon. Orphaned at two years old, Youseff was raised by his uncle and entered the monastery at the age of twenty-three. He was drawn to the monastic life, meaning that he lived alone and according to a rule that included taking vows of poverty, chastity, and obedience. Youseff also took the new name "Charbel" after a great second-century martyr. He was instructed by Father Nimatullah (who later became Saint Hardini), was eventually ordained a priest in 1859, and spent the next sixteen years of his life living humbly, working hard, and praying with great discipline. During this time, however, Charbel longed to live in even stricter silence and in total abandonment to God. It was at this point that Charbel took "roughing it" to a whole new level.

Charbel lived as a hermit for the next twenty-three years, until his death. He kept a strict fast. He spent most of his day in the presence of the Blessed Sacrament. He slept on a slab of stone with a half stump of wood for his pillow. The hermitage in which he lived was almost a mile above sea level, nestled in the snow-covered mountains – and Charbel's cell had neither a heater or blankets. (How's that for roughing it?) Through his personal daily prayer and penance, he offered himself as a sacrifice for all, praying that the world would return to God. He endured frequent hunger, poverty, physical fatigue, and unbearable cold with the unflinching courage of a martyr.

This meek monk wielded great power in his humility and holiness. He once rescued fellow monks from a deadly snake simply by asking the snake to go away. When a swarm of locusts was destroying local crops, promising widespread local famine, Charbel was asked to bless the fields. No sooner had the monk broken out the holy water than the locusts fled and every single remaining crop was saved. It's said, too, that when Charbel anointed a young boy dying of typhus with the Sacrament of the Sick, he immediately returned to perfect health. One mentally-ill man even regained his lucidity and sanity by kneeling in front of the Blessed Sacrament while Charbel read to him from the Gospel.

When Charbel finally died, following a stroke on Christmas Eve in 1898, the monks rushed to his bedside, hoping to be blessed by him one last time. What followed after his death left even the monks (who'd taken a vow of silence) speechless.

After he was buried, great light of dazzling beauty and extraordinary brightness began emanating from Charbel's modest grave; it cut through the darkness of night and could be seen from a great distance. The holy "night light" continued for forty-five days after his death.

When Charbel's body was exhumed and examined in detail, it was noticed that his corpse was secreting both sweat and blood yet showed no signs of deterioration. Each of the four times his grave has been opened by official committees, his body has demonstrated the same miraculous traits and is as flexible today as when he was still alive. Countless pilgrims have been blessed enough to pray near Charbel and to ask for his intercession. Pope Pius XI began his canonization process in 1925, and in 1977, little Youseff was canonized Saint Charbel (of Lebanon) by Pope Paul VI.

A humble and holy man of God, Saint Charbel's life is proof that all we need is God. If your prayer life needs a boost, if your life has become too noisy, or if you feel tethered by your cell phone, laptop, or flat screen, why not ask Saint Charbel to pray with you and for you? His intercession will not only help you simplify your life, but also provide that "night light" in the midst of modern cultural darkness.

Saint Christina the Astonishing

Feast day: July 24th

Patron of: mental health caregivers, mental health professionals, mentally ill people, psychiatrists, and therapists

Invoked against: mental disorders and mental illness

It must have been difficult for people to figure out what "title" to give Saint Christina before finally settling on "the Astonishing." Reading through her life, it's obvious that several titles could have been considered, like "Christina the Invincible," or "Christina the Unbreakable," or even "Christina the Bloodhound." Are you confused? So were most of the people who knew Saint Christina.

Christina never lived what you would call a "normal life." She was born into a peasant family and orphaned at a young age, and her two older sisters raised her. Now, before you go thinking that this sounds like some overdramatic Dickens novel, know that this is probably the most normal part of her life. Born in the twelfth century, much of what we know about Christina comes by way of testimony, eyewitness accounts, and legend.

After suffering a severe seizure at about twenty-one years old, Christina was pronounced dead. Some believe she may have just fallen into a cataleptic state (go ahead and look that up if you want) and was thus "believed" to be dead. In either case, what happened next is straight out of *Saturday Night Live*. In front of dozens of witnesses, Christina **sat up in her coffin** during her own funeral Mass (and just in case you're thinking that this is easily explained through a misdiagnosis of death, wait until you hear what happened next). Christina then *flew* up into the rafters of the church (some say she levitated, others that she shot forth like an arrow), from where she refused to come down because the stench of the people's sin was apparently too repugnant to bear. When she was eventually "ordered" down by the priest, she landed on the altar, stepped down, and told those remaining (the few who hadn't run out in fear) of how she had been to hell, Purgatory, and heaven before returning from the dead. She stated that she had chosen to return to earth with a specific ministry to pray and encourage prayer for all of the souls trapped in Purgatory.

The events of Christina's life in the decades that followed were equally "astonishing." Her strong sense of smell was a constant battle for her; Christina was literally able to smell the sin of those around her. The odor was so repugnant that she would constantly climb trees, hide in cupboards or large ovens, and even levitate just to avoid contact with sinful people. It's reported that she could handle fire – even roll in it – without the least bit of harm. Freezing water was not a problem for the saint, either; it's said that Christina stood in a frozen winter lake for hours without any harm coming to her. So inexplicable was her saintly invincibility and miraculous – albeit strange – stories of the afterlife that some tried to have her committed to an asylum. They even tried chaining her to a pillar, from which she "somehow" escaped. Some accused her of being a demon. Others thought her strictly insane. Countless souls, though, came to her for her wisdom and advice.

A Dominican professor of theology, who knew Christina personally, documented her miraculous life and strange abilities, adding eyewitness testimonies to abolish most concerns about this story being pure legend. The prioress at Christina's convent also praised the saint, saying that she was always obedient and quite holy. So, while some called her crazy, many closest to her praised her Catholicism. Fittingly, she is now the patron saint of psychiatrists.

Christina dedicated her life to God, living in absolute

poverty and praying for the dead to be reunited with Christ in heaven. Perhaps we should suggest yet another title: "Saint Christina the Insanely Awesome." Ask Saint Christina to pray with you for a heightened awareness of sin and a more ardent desire to avoid it. If we all feared and avoided sin with Saint Christina's energy, countless more souls would enjoy the splendors of heaven.

Saint Christopher

Feast day: July 25th

Patron of: archers, automobile drivers, motorists, travelers, truck drivers.

Invoked against: bad dreams, epilepsy, floods, hailstorms, lightning, pestilence, storms, sudden death, and toothaches.

Heroes can have a lot of qualities, but one that's universally needed is strength. If there was ever a strong man you'd need to carry your team to victory, Saint Christopher would be the guy. But this third century holy man has caused quite a bit of controversy in the time since his death.

Christopher wasn't born with that name; he was born in Canaan (a name you may recognize from the Old Testament) with the name Offerus. In the midst of a pagan culture, Christopher's mother was a converted Christian who conceived after asking for the intercession of Mary. Her prayer worked overtime – tradition tells us that Offerus grew to be over seven feet tall and was extremely strong. Once he grew up, the now-giant man set out on a mission: to serve the strongest king he could find.

At first, Offerus served the king of Canaan, but then found a mightier king and left to serve him. That king, however, was afraid of another – he feared the devil, and crossed himself when Satan's name was mentioned. Offerus took this as a sign that the devil was a greater king than his current master, and set out to find Satan. While traveling, he ran into evil men, one of whom claimed to *be* the devil. Offerus then served *that* man, until one day they came upon a cross. The evil man fled at the sight of the cross, and Offerus knew he had to, yet again, search for the mightiest king.

A Christian hermit lived nearby, and Offerus asked him about the cross. The hermit explained what it was, and told him that he'd have to begin praying if he was going to serve Christ. This next part might be unique, especially to saints: Offerus told him no. He couldn't pray and he would not fast, but he could serve. He told the hermit he would carry travelers across the river safely as a way to serve Christ.

The funny thing about God is that he *created* humor ... so you get one guess as to who Offerus' most famous passenger was. A child came to the bank of the river; as Offerus carried him, the child got heavier and heavier, until it felt like the entire planet was on his shoulders. Then the child revealed to Offerus that he was Christ, who carried the weight of the whole world. The man from Canaan pledged his life, and was baptized by Christ in the same river he served in.

He took the name "Christopher," which means – you guessed it – "Christ bearer." After becoming a Christian, he converted many souls with his simple witness. The local king wasn't too happy about this, so he came and offered Christopher whatever it would take to win back his loyalty. But Christopher was already serving the King of Kings, and when he refused to deny his faith, he was beheaded.

So what's the controversy over this giant of the faith? Well, back before we had Church councils and teams of investigators to discover the lives of saints, popular demand could put someone onto the list. Christopher's story and legend grew so much that he quickly became a famous saint throughout the Christian world. But centuries later, when the Church began investigating the stories of the early saints, legend was all they could find about Christopher. Many of the stories of his life closely followed similar stories from other saints or mythical characters, and it wasn't clear which version was the original – or if any of them truly happened. In 1969, Christopher was taken off the official calendar of Catholic saints (meaning he no longer gets "headliner" status on his own feast day playbill), but he is still recognized as a saint of the Church. Devotion and prayers for his intercession are still strong around the world, as he's the patron saint of all travelers.

If you're looking for a holy card of Saint Christopher, don't be thrown off if you see a dog's head staring back at you. In some versions of his life story the word "Canaanite" was mistranslated; so instead of it meaning he was from Canaan, it read that he had the head of a *canis* – also known as a dog.

Whether or not Saint Christopher, as described here, lived the life people say he did, or was as physically imposing as legend tells us, we can all agree that strength is something every Christian soul needs. You can be confident in asking the saints, including Saint Christopher, to pray with you for increased strength in the face of persecution, temptation, or suffering – they've been through it all. The more you ask, in prayer, for the Holy Spirit to unleash your inner strength and virtue, the more you become a "Christopher" (Christ-bearer) to the world.

Saint Clare of Assisi

Feast day: August 11th

Patron of: eyes, laundry workers, telephones, television, and television writers

Invoked against: eye disease

Do you remember when you were a kid and you'd get into an argument with your parents, and then tell them you were going to run away from home? Did you ever think about where you were going to *go* when you left? Saint Clare of Assisi did, and it led to a life of powerful miracles for the Kingdom of God.

The daughter of an Italian count, Clare had money and status in a world where those two keys opened all the doors...but that wasn't enough. From childhood, she shunned the ways of the world and embraced the simplicity of Christ. At age eighteen, when she heard Saint Francis preaching (yep, the animal-loving, order-starting Francis), she decided to follow his example of selling everything and serving God. She soon started an order of women religious; when her sister Agnes tried to join, the girls' father was fed up. He sent a dozen men to haul Agnes back to the family home, but when Clare prayed for her, Agnes became so heavy that the twelve men couldn't budge her (guess her heavenly Father wanted her in His house a little more). Eventually Clare's other sister and her mother joined the order.

The sisters lived a life of such extreme simplicity that when Pope Gregory IX visited Clare, he offered to absolve her vow of poverty. She kindly refused, saying that the only thing she wanted absolution from was sin (that's got to be in the top five saintly zingers, right?).

One night, an army of soldiers that was tearing through Italy came to her convent and was ready to break down the gates. What did this former noblewoman and future saint do? She got out of bed, went to the tabernacle, and brought the Blessed Sacrament out to the top of the front gate in a monstrance. Kneeling, she asked God to protect her sisters – and He responded (God's cool like that). As Clare lifted the Eucharist, the army was thrown into a panicked frenzy and retreated, leaving the sisters safe. It was true then and it's true now: don't mess with nuns.

As Clare grew older, she fell ill and at one point could not get out of bed for Mass. Missing Mass was a no-go for Clare, and she was granted a miracle: during the Liturgy, an image of what was going on would appear on the wall of her cell. Because of this paschal projection, Clare is the patron saint of television. That means the first television show was Mass – something we should keep in mind while that remote's in our hand.

It's often easier to talk about what you believe than it is to act on it; Saint Clare did both. She didn't just talk the talk – she walked the walk. Invite her to pray with you, asking her to help you see all the areas of your life that keep you from being completely sold-out for Christ. When God reveals those areas to you, ask Saint Clare of Assisi to pray for you, that you would have the reckless abandon for God that she had. Who knows? Perhaps you can be the patron saint of HD television ... that spot hasn't been filled yet.

Saints Cosmas & Damian

Feast day: September 26th

Patrons of: physicians, surgeons, doctors, chemical workers, and barbers.

Peanut butter and jelly, macaroni and cheese, thunder and lightning...some things just "go together." Such is the case for many Catholics who hear the word "Cosmas" and immediately follow it up with "and Damian." These twin brothers made quite a name for themselves among their peers and, as a result of their great holiness, are still being celebrated centuries later.

Born in Arabia and trained as doctors, the twins were constantly broke because they never charged people for their services ... not exactly a *prescription* for success but, nonetheless, their unmatched benevolence and great charity won countless hearts for the Lord.

Some found their medical practices a bit odd, but no one could argue with their effectiveness. One of their most popular methods of treatment, known as "incubation," encouraged patients to sleep in a church in the presence of the Blessed Sacrament until they were miraculously cured.

Tradition and numerous legends tell of miraculous feats wrought at the hands of these wonder-working brothers. When one man had a snake slither into his mouth and infest his body, Cosmas and Damian prayed over him, only to watch as the snake slithered out and fled. When a diseased man lost his lower leg, Cosmas and Damian successfully performed what was apparently the world's first unofficial transplant, grafting a healthy leg in its place. The fact that the patient was white and the donor black only furthered the story's fame, in a time and region where racial inequality flourished.

Accused of witchcraft and sorcery, they were sentenced to death by a local judge and condemned to be thrown into the sea. An angel of the Lord arrived to fish them out of the sea and return them to ... the judge.

At that point you have to wonder what the brothers were thinking ... "Umm, thanks?"

The judge, upon seeing their miraculous return, then renounced his own witchcraft and proclaimed he would convert to Catholicism. At that moment, two demons appeared and began beating the judge. Cosmas and Damian began praying earnestly and then watched as the demons fled and the judge was restored to perfect health.

The judge then renounced his renouncement (didn't he ever hear about the "no take back-sies" rule?), fearful of what following Christ would entail. Expressing that he did not want to be tormented again, he then had Cosmas and Damian thrown into a fire. An angel of the Lord appeared to rescue them from the fire. Shocked but not to be outdone, the judge then commanded the brothers to be thrown into prison, shot with arrows, and stoned to death. How's that for overkill? (Pardon the pun.)

The brothers were not harmed at all. In fact, witnesses reported that the brothers' prayers apparently caused the arrows and stones to boomerang back at their executioners, killing them on contact.

Cosmas and Damian were eventually beheaded and buried together. The Church venerates these beloved saints and even lists them in the prayers of communion (Eucharistic Prayer One). While some historians proclaim that the brothers were not real – only modern versions of Castor and Pollux of Greek mythological fame – countless souls have been blessed by their intercession and they remain patrons for surgeons, doctors, chemical workers, and barbers. Yes, barbers, which is ironic given that they lost their heads in martyrdom.

If you ever get "too logical" or find yourself in those philosophical debates about God and science with people who struggle to believe or who seem to be without faith, ask Saints Cosmas and Damian to pray with you. Ask the Lord to grant you the same courage and vindication in the face of trials and indictments from non-believers of the modern, "scientific" age. And the next time you head to the barber or, heaven forbid, in for surgery, thank God for the gift of these holy brothers who, although they pioneered amputation, were forced to live in an age before peanut butter and jelly. Perish the thought!

Saint Dominic

Feast day: August 8th

Patron of: astronomers, astronomy, falsely accused people, and scientists

There are some saints who we know little about, and others whose legacies could fill entire books – Saint Dominic is definitely in the second category. Dominic had a life packed with so many amazing stories that it's hard to know what to say ... a problem that he never had. The story of Saint Dominic is one of a man who is the official poster boy for Luke 21:15 (yes, this means you have to look it up – go dust off your Bible!).

Before Dominic was even born, God told people he would do great things. His mother Juana (who later also became a saint) had a vision while she was pregnant with him. She saw, instead of her son, a dog with a flaming torch in its mouth that was setting the whole world on fire for God – a foreshadowing of how powerful Dominic's words would be. When Dominic was baptized, Juana saw a star brightly shining from her son's chest – a miracle that would later cause him to be known as the patron saint of astronomers.

As a young man, Dominic was extremely virtuous – he even sold his schoolbooks so that he could use the money to feed the poor, and he also tried to ransom himself as a trade to free some slaves. When he became a priest, Dominic's passion was to preach to heretics and convert them to Christ, and he was famous for being unstoppable in debates against unbelievers. At the age of forty-six, Dominic created the Order of Preachers – commonly known now as the Dominicans. The Dominicans are sometimes jokingly called "the Lord's dogs," not because of the vision of the dog with the torch but because the Latin word for Lord is *Dominus* and the Latin word for dog is *canis*.

When Dominic was asked to become a bishop, his response was simple: God made him to preach, not to be a bishop. Dominic's straight-shooting response worked; he was never made a bishop. Instead, he and his order traveled throughout Europe battling Albigensianism (a heresy saying that everything material is evil). He wrote treatises explaining the problems with the heresy, and during an argument, his work was thrown into a fire along with books supporting Albigensianism. The heretical books burned, but Dominic's book was undamaged. They even fished it out and threw it in a few more times to see if it would burn, and still nothing happened. (Holy book burning, Batman!)

During their travels, Muslim pirates took Dominic and his brothers captive. Little did the pirates know that God's a big fan of miracles in the ocean. Soon the boat was in the middle of an enormous storm; Dominic preached, telling the pirates to ask for the intercession of Mary and to put their faith in Christ. They ignored him ... the first two times. The third time Dominic asked, the pirates were converted, and the storm ceased.

Words weren't the only thing Dominic gave to the Church – in a moment of deep despair, the holy priest cried out to Mary for help. She appeared to Dominic, giving him a set of roses that represented the Rosary. To this day, the Dominican order spreads Our Lady's prayer throughout the world.

If you've ever been in a position where God asked you to share your faith, you know it can be a little scary. Those moments when we know that we need to say something, to stick our neck out and proclaim God's truth, can be some of the most uncomfortable in our faith. Don't be afraid to ask Saint Dominic when you need to talk to strangers. He once had a vision of a beggar who he knew would do great things for God. The next day, he ran into that beggar – a man we've come to know as Saint Francis of Assisi.

Saint Dominic Savio

Feast day: March 9th

Patron of: boys, children's choirs, choirs, falsely accused people, and juvenile delinquents

Long before the success of *Glee*, being known as a "choir boy" was usually a negative thing. Not only was Saint Dominic Savio a choir boy, he's even the patron saint of them. In his short, saintly life, Dominic became an altar boy at age five and entered a preparatory school at twelve with dreams of becoming a priest.

Mentored by Saint John Bosco (whom you'll also read about in this book), Dominic Savio was one of those souls who seemed almost too good to be true. His purity gained the attention of everyone around him; even his classmates, who found his holiness to be a bit overbearing at times.

Once, when other boys began fighting on the playground, Dominic quickly grabbed a crucifix and inserted himself between the young pugilists; he went on to preach to his peers about the sin of violence and the call to love one another. Dominic would have made a great hall monitor or safety patrol.

Dominic was always looking out for the well-being – both physical and spiritual – of the other boys in John Bosco's care. Once when some of the boys were looking at pornography, Dominic discovered them, quickly grabbed the materials, and shredded them so that they would not fall any deeper into sin. He was so in love with the Lord that even in the midst of playing ball with his friends in the courtyard, Dominic would sometimes pause midgame, unable to move, while he had a vision of heaven opening above him. The young mystic's visions were so powerful that Saint John Bosco had him share them with the Pope.

When Dominic's mother was in great pain during her pregnancy with his sister, he merely hugged and kissed her and her pain reportedly left, not to return. Tales of Dominic's holiness spread throughout the region long after he fell ill and died at the age of fifteen. After Dominic's death, he appeared to his grieving mother to assure her that he was, indeed, in heaven. The ceiling of the room she was in opened up and there was Dominic in the midst of dazzling light, easing his mother's mourning and drying her tears. It's likely that no teenage son in history has ever loved his mother quite like that.

John Bosco's biography of Dominic is the most trustworthy account of the young saint's inspiring life, an eyewitness testimony to how boldly the love and power of God can move through even a young teenager. To date, Dominic holds the record for the youngest saint not martyred for the faith. You can visit his tomb in the basilica of Mary, Help of Christians in Turin, not far from the tomb of his mentor and teacher, Saint John Bosco.

If you've ever been mocked for being "too holy" or been accused of being "holier than thou" (which would be a great title for a book), know that you're in good company with Saint Dominic Savio. This "Mama's boy" and "choir boy" may have been mocked and even found a little over-bearing by some of his peers, but his love for the Lord and for his family earned him great favor with God and the Church. Over one hundred and fifty years later we're still talking about this teenage saint, and the Church will be talking about him for hundreds of years to come. Quite a legacy left in just fifteen years, huh?

Saint Dorothy

Feast day: February 6th

Patron of: brewers, brides, florists, gardeners, midwives, and newlyweds

When you say the name "Dorothy," most immediately think of the "merry 'ol land of Oz," where a gentle and humble young farm girl befriends misfits and battles a wicked witch. And while that Dorothy is heroic, she cannot begin to hold a torch to her namesake, *Saint* Dorothy.

Our story begins far under the rainbow, in the Middle East – Caesarea of Cappadocia, to be exact. Dorothy was known for her great beauty and holiness. The young virgin was so breathtaking that many men sought her attention, most notably the local provost named Fabricus. When he proposed marriage (and if she refused, death), Saint Dorothy lovingly proposed he take a walk, telling him, "Christ [was her] only spouse and death [her] desire."

Fabricus, still wanting to marry her, then sent two women (who'd fallen away from the faith) to plead his case, in hopes of "turning her to the dark side." In turn, Dorothy converted both women; the love for Christ that burned in her heart reignited their own. These successful conversions earned her time on "the rack," and she was painfully stretched out over flames. Dorothy smiled during the torturous exercise and joyfully exclaimed, "I have brought back two souls to Christ and I shall soon be in heaven rejoicing with the angels." Dorothy's rejoicing grew even stronger as she was struck repeatedly in the face and burned with red-hot irons.

It didn't stop there, either. (Dorothy would have been the last one standing in the Ultimate Fighting Challenge.) The authorities threw her in jail and angels fed her. They threw her into oil – and it miraculously turned into balm. No matter what they tried, they just couldn't seem to break her spirit or to kill this holy woman of God. They sentenced her to death, by beheading – and Dorothy rejoiced that Jesus, the "Lover of [her] soul, had invited [her] into the nuptial chamber." There was no need to click heels together or seek a wizard for help; for Dorothy, death by martyrdom was nothing to fear and everything to celebrate. This is why Dorothy is the patroness of brides while also simultaneously invoked against fire.

On the way to her beheading, a pagan lawyer named Theophilus told her, mockingly, to "send him fruit and flowers from her heavenly garden." After Dorothy's death, an angel disguised as a child reportedly showed up at his doorstop carrying three apples and three roses. The fruit and flowers were apparently so beautiful and their aroma so heavenly that it was evident that they could not have been grown on earth. Theophilus converted almost immediately, was then executed, cut into pieces, and fed to the animals, sharing in Dorothy's martyrdom.

Stories like these of Saint Dorothy and Theophilus remind us that the "happy ending" of life doesn't always occur on earth. When you're fearful of what following the Lord might require you to do, ask Saint Dorothy to pray with you. Living out your faith boldly and joyfully in the face of persecution might not bring a fairy tale ending on earth, but as we see in the case of Saint Dorothy, the happy ending will one day occur when you will assuredly receive a round of applause in heaven, which is much higher, more beautiful, and more Godly than the wonderful land of Oz. Oh, and if you were hoping for a rainbow story, see Genesis chapters 6-9 (where you can also learn about the world's first houseboat).

Saint Felix of Nola

Feast day: January 14th

Patron of: domestic animals and eyes

Invoked against: eye disease, eye trouble, false witness, lies, and perjury

If the saints who fly (levitate) are the Catholic Church's version of Superman, then "The Amazing Spiderman" would undoubtedly be Saint Felix of Nola.

Felix was the son of a Roman soldier and grew up on his father's estate in Nola, Italy (near Naples). Upon his father's death, Felix gave away all of his earthly possessions to the poor and was ordained a priest by Bishop Saint Maximus (of Nola). Felix then became the assistant (and student) of the bishop, helping him minister to Christians in a time when it wasn't safe to be one.

Soon after Felix's ordination (in about 250 AD), the emperor at the time, Decius, waged a horrific and bloody war on the Catholic (Christian) Church, seizing and murdering countless souls during what is now historically called the "Decian Persecution." The bishop was forced to flee into the desert; Felix was arrested and imprisoned in the place of the bishop, and was tortured for his beliefs. One night, an angel appeared to Felix in prison and freed him – in typical "Acts of the Apostles" style (Acts chapters 5, 12, and 16), his chains fell off and the cell door opened.

What happened next is the stuff legends (and comic books) are made of. As Felix was running from a pursuing army of guards, he ducked down a crowded city street into a small, cave-like "opening" in the wall. Upon entering it, a spider began rapidly spinning a web back and forth across the entrance to Felix's hiding place. So quickly and furiously did the miraculous spider work that when the pursuant enemy passed by the opening, the spider's web gave the impression that it could not have been entered for quite some time.

After his harrowing escape, Felix fulfilled the jailbreak angel's instructions to find and help his bishop, Saint Maximus, who had grown quite sick. Felix brought his mentor back to Nola to care for him and, upon the bishop's death; the people unanimously selected Felix to replace him. Felix, however, filled with humility, declined the honor and asked for an "older and wiser" priest to assume the role instead.

Felix spent the remaining decades of his life working tirelessly for the poor; he was so beloved and celebrated that his tomb became not only a popular destination for prayer but also the sight of countless healings and miracles. Multiple saints wrote about this holy man of God, and five churches were built in his honor, yet most people today have never heard of him.

Ask Saint Felix to pray with you and for you, that you would never lose heart or doubt God's faithfulness even when the situation looks bad. God is faithful until the end. As Felix, the Catholic "Spider-man," reminds us, "Where God is, a spider's web is a wall. Where He is not, a wall is but spider's web."

Saint Francis of Assisi

Feast day: October 4th

Patron of: animals, environmentalism, families, merchants, peace, zoos, Italy, and the Franciscan Order

Invoked against: dying alone and fire

Few saints enjoy the kind of "rock star" status that Saint Francis of Assisi does. Since his death in 1226, countless souls have been challenged by his holy example and countless gardens have displayed statues in his honor. It's kind of ironic, if you think about it ... there's Saint Francis, known for his love of animals, now serving as a target for pigeons everywhere. Still, Saint Francis was so humble even he probably would have thought it was funny.

Francis of Assisi was born in 1181 in, you guessed it, Assisi – a little town in northern Italy. The son of a very wealthy cloth merchant, he was a wild child and lived a pretty crazy young adulthood by most peoples' accounts. He joined the army, fought in the fourth Crusade, and was intent on becoming a knight. He was captured soon after he joined and spent a year in prison before eventually being ransomed.

Not long after that, upon his return to Assisi, he was moved with pity toward a leper. He gave the man his cloak and even kissed his wounds. Something was happening in Francis' heart. At the age of 26, while praying before the crucifix in an old, rundown chapel, he heard a voice from the crucifix say to him, "Francis, repair my church, which has fallen into disrepair, as you can see." Francis took the words literally and quickly began "fixing" the dilapidated building. In time, Francis came to understand that the Lord was talking about rebuilding the greater, universal Church, not just the chapel building.

Francis went forth with nothing earthly to his name. He traveled the countryside, begging and preaching the gospel message. Most people ridiculed him, but a small group that also renounced their possessions began to travel with him. Within about fifteen years, he was leading over 5,000 friars and an order of religious sisters (the Poor Clares, begun by Saint Clare of Assisi). He crafted a strict rule of life to live by which called for absolute poverty, authentic humility, and great discipline. This rule (which is still followed today) led the Franciscans and their founder to great holiness.

Though he wrote beautiful prayers and was a gentle and compassionate soul, this man from Assisi was not a sissy. He preached against greed and worldly excess to a world (and even some of the Church) that didn't want to hear it. He would sit on a jagged rock while he meditated on the Passion of our Lord. He went without food for himself while giving what little he had to others. Through prayer he drew water from a stone to offer drink to a thirsty beggar. He had a vision of an angel so powerful he was knocked to the ground and burned with its angelic rays.

People know of Francis' great love for animals, but few understand just how close he was to them. It's said that when this great saint preached, the birds would fall silent and listen, in front of witnesses. When a savage wolf was terrorizing and killing townspeople outside of Assisi, Francis tamed the beast. He taught boldly about the gift of God's creation, believing that everything reflected the Creator's love for us; which is why he is, among several other things, the patron saint of ecology.

His Franciscan brothers reported witnessing incredible miracles while in his presence over the years, including watching him levitate, bilocate, heal paralytics, and cleanse lepers of their leprosy. He is said to have cured those who were mute, deaf, and blind and to have even exorcised demons from people who were possessed simply by walking into the room they were in. One monk watched as Francis conversed with Jesus Christ, the Blessed Virgin Mary, and Saint John the Baptist in visions during his night prayer. Francis asked the monk not to share this instance and, obviously, the monk disobeyed, since we're discussing it here.

And as if this weren't enough, while praying in 1224, Francis was granted the gift of the stigmata – the marks of Christ's five wounds – upon his own body, which bled for the remaining two years of his life.

Strive to approach not only the Creator (God) but also His creation as Saint Francis did. Encounter nature. Care for the earth. Thank God for the animals, whether it's the dog you're playing with or the chicken you're eating for dinner. Seek to love God above all other things and you'll find, as Saint Francis did, that things have a way of working out (Romans 8:28).

Saint Gall

Feast day: October 16th

Patron of: birds, geese, and poultry

If you're Irish (or claim to be), you probably have Saint Patrick on your list of patron saints. Well, surprise, surprise: Saint Patrick wasn't Irish (we know you're heartbroken, but check out the whole story). Although Patrick only spent time in Ireland, it turns out there were a few saints who were natives of the land of rolling hills and four-leaf clovers.

One of those lesser-known Irish saints was Saint Gall, who grew up in an Irish monastery in the middle 500s. He was close with some older saints, including Saint Columban. As Gall got older, the two men became traveling companions as they went to different lands to spread the Gospel. Gall followed Columban to France, where they worked for a few years until the king forced them to leave. The two men then headed to Bregentz, a town on the Swiss/Austrian border. Columban soon moved on; Gall stayed and preached to the heretics, but the crowds weren't always pleased by his words. As he spoke, three of the statues to false gods in the city broke into pieces, and Gall threw them into the lake. He then took over a chapel full of idols and dedicated it to a martyr, Saint Aurelia.

As Gall spent more time with the people of the region, God started using him for more and more miracles. He cast out demons, converted crowds, and even drove snakes from the valley (Is that just an Irish saint thing? Do they all do that?). When the fiancé of the king was possessed, Gall exorcised the demons from her ... it's even said that blackbirds flew out of the woman's mouth.

Gall was always at peace with animals (aside from the times they represented demonic possession, of course). He even received help within the animal kingdom from time to time: once, when Gall was camping with brothers in the woods, he told a nearby bear to bring him firewood. The bear actually brought it, which is why Saint Gall has one of the coolest images in his saintly icons: a bear with a log in its mouth.

God called Saint Gall into some pretty scary territory and placed him in very challenging situations, but God never left him abandoned. Do you ever fear doing what the Lord asks because a situation looks impossible or frightens you? If so, ask Saint Gall to pray with you. The Lord does not set you up to fail (1 Corinthians 10:13) and He will never abandon you. God will take you by the hand (Isaiah 41:10) and lead you to victory, if you let Him.

Saint Gerard Majella

Feast day: October 16th

Patron of: childbirth, expectant mothers, falsely accused people, lay brothers, the pro-life movement, and unborn children

The dozens of saints listed in this book (and countless saints who are not) were capable, by the power of God, of doing miraculous things, things that the human mind can scarcely fathom. These incredible feats of supernatural power are a testament not only to God but also to what can happen when a soul is completely abandoned to the love of God – sustained by the Holy Spirit. Few saints left more of his peers dumbfounded, muttering, "How'd he do that?" than Saint Gerard Majella.

Born in 1726 near Naples, Gerard's youth was spent supporting and caring for his widowed mother and siblings. It's said that as a five-year-old boy he would visit the local chapel daily to pray. Every day Gerard would inexplicably return with loaves of bread to feed his family. When asked where he got them, Gerard replied that "a most beautiful boy" had given them to him. One day, his sister accompanied him to the chapel where she witnessed Gerard in prayer – kneeling before a statue of the Blessed Virgin Mary holding the Child Jesus and interacting with them. The Child Jesus apparently left His Mother's arms, began to play with Gerard, and miraculously gave him loaves of bread.

As if that display were not enough proof of Gerard's great holiness, once, when he desired to receive Communion but was refused because he was not yet old enough, Gerard prayed so earnestly that Saint Michael the Archangel brought him the Eucharist to receive. Yes, you read that correctly. When Saint Michael is your private Eucharistic Minister, you've got game. Saint Michael would appear to him – and even to those with him – at various other times throughout this saint's life.

At twenty-three years old Gerard became a professed brother in the Redemptorist order. Though not a priest, Gerard was asked to offer spiritual direction and counsel to communities of nuns. His great wisdom and true piety were often overshadowed, however, by the miracles so many witnessed through him. Countless reports came in from people who'd witnessed Gerard do things no one could explain outside of the power of God. Gerard could read the secret sins on peoples' souls. He could levitate and even fly. He had the ability to become invisible at will. He brought a boy who'd fallen off a cliff back to life. Witnesses watched as he walked across water to help a boatload of fishermen survive a terrible storm. When a plague broke out in his town, Gerard bilocated to several different houses, helping the sick and those who were shut-in.

When the miracles became too much for some to bear, his Superior ordered him to stop performing miracles without first asking for permission. Not long after, a man fell from a building and Gerard told the man – in mid-air – to stop falling. The man did, hovering above the ground. Gerard then asked his Superior if he was allowed to save the falling man. His Superior agreed and Gerard, having obediently sought permission, gently guided the man to the ground safely.

Once he accidentally left his handkerchief behind at a house he was visiting. Noticing the lost article, the daughter of the house grabbed it and ran to catch up with the saint, who replied, "Keep it, it may be useful to you someday." Years later as the daughter – now grown – was dying in childbirth, she remembered the handkerchief. After it was brought to her she invoked Gerard's intercession; she recovered and gave birth to a healthy baby. It's for this reason that Gerard is the patron saint of childbirth and expectant mothers.

After his death in 1755, the entire Monastery in which he died was filled with an indescribably sweet odor that lasted for several days. His remains were processed through nearby towns and villages where numerous people – including one young girl who suffered from tuberculosis of the bone – were instantaneously healed as his body passed by.

If you ever wonder if miracles still happen, Saint Gerard's life is tremendous and substantial proof that they do. More importantly, his example reminds us that God is very active among and within His children. Faith does not contradict reason; it exceeds it. The question is not whether God answers prayers but whether our prayers are to fulfill God's will or our own agendas. Saint Gerard Majella lived for God and, in doing so, became living proof that the Creator works well beyond the limits of creation, if we let Him.

Saint Giles

Feast day: September 1st

Patron of: beggars, blacksmiths, breast-feeding, cancer patients, disabled people, epileptics, and the mentally ill

Invoked against: breast cancer, epilepsy, fear of night, leprosy, and mental illness

Some of the saints you'll read about in this book had one huge miracle; there was one gift, one grace, one attribute that they'll always be remembered for. Saint Giles breaks out of that mold with a life that could honestly give him the title of "Miracle Machine."

Although he was born into money, his heart would soon rest with the poor. When he was still young, Giles ran into a poor, sick beggar on the road. So he did what Christ has asked all of us to do when we meet the poor – Giles gave the man his coat. When the beggar put on the coat, he was instantly healed and healthy – a miracle that fixated Giles on a life of simplicity and poverty. He sold all he had after the death of his parents and became a hermit, retreating from the world to pray.

But good news travels fast, and whenever Giles ran into people in need, miracles happened. Big miracles. He cured the sick, cast out demons, stopped tempests in the sea, and even raised a prince from the dead. Every time Giles would perform a miracle, more people would seek him out, and he would retreat farther into forests and deserts. It seems it's true what they say: more miracles, more problems.

Eventually, Giles was deep in the woods away from

civilization. He was living like a Catholic *Man vs. Wild*, eating berries and herbs to stay alive. At times, a hind (which you might know as a deer) would come and help take care of him, giving him milk to drink. Because he was a hermit, the hind was his only companion, and one day a group of hunters and their dogs had their targets set on this particular animal.

Giles was distressed, and prayed that God would take care of the animal that had taken care of him. Suddenly the hind appeared, laying itself at the feet of the hermit in his cave. The hunters outside tried to scare it by shooting an arrow into the cave, but the arrow hit Giles in the hand instead. When the men realized they had shot a holy man, they apologized (that had to be awkward) and went back to relay the story to the king. Amazed, the king brought the bishop with him to meet this solitary man of God, and Giles was ordained a priest. He refused medicine for his hand, and the wound never healed – a constant reminder of the miracle God had done. (That'd beat out other cool "scar stories" any day.)

As a priest, Giles was obedient to the bishop's request that he live in a monastery instead of the woods. His reputation preceded him, and the emperor Charlemagne asked Giles to say a Mass for his sins ... but there was one sin he felt was too awful to confess. During the Mass, an angel flew over the altar and dropped a letter in front of Giles. It contained Charlemagne's un-confessed sin.

Angelic letters weren't the only thing divinely mailed to Giles during his priesthood. When the Pope gave him two large cypress doors to put on the front of his monastery, Giles realized he had no way to transport them (one of the things that happens in a holy life of extreme poverty). Trusting God's providence, he threw the doors into the Tiber River and asked the Lord to send them where they were meant to go. When he returned to his monastery, the doors were there – leaning up against the wall. By land or by sea (or by angel), God really has the best messengers.

Saint Giles easily could have used the gifts (and miracles) that God granted him for his own glory, but he did not. Have you ever struggled in this area? Do you look for affirmation or attention for those talents or skills God gave you to build His Kingdom, rather than your own? Everyone struggles with this from time to time. Ask Saint Giles to pray with you for greater humility, asking God to reveal to you all of the ways He wants to use the gifts He has given you to – like Saint Giles – lead other souls to Heaven.

Saint Helena

Feast day: August 18th

Patron of: archeologists, converts, difficult marriages, divorced people, and empresses

As you look through the lives of the saints, you'll notice that a lot of them can fall into similar categories: visionaries, preachers, healers, servants, martyrs – the list just goes on and on. But Saint Helena might be the only saint who was like a real-life Indiana Jones, with a story that's unique even for *this* book.

Helena caught the attention of the Roman emperor Constantius, and later gave birth to a son named Constantine – the same Constantine who founded the Holy Roman Empire. But having a powerful son is only a small part of Helena's saintly legacy.

Late in her life, Helena converted to Christianity – some reports say she converted her son to the faith; others say it was vice versa. (Odds are she converted her son – there is no force on earth more powerful than a mother who prays.) Either way, once she was devoted to Christ, Helena used every resource at her disposal for God's glory. She gave away large amounts of money and other resources to the churches she would visit, dressing as a commoner and praying with local communities.

Helena traveled to the Holy Land in search of relics, and she found a lot of them. As she journeyed through the land Christ walked in his earthly life, she built churches at the sites of the Nativity, the Ascension, and even the spot where Moses talked to the burning bush. When Helena found the site of Christ's tomb, she discovered that a temple to a pagan god had been built over it.

Here's a lesson: don't get between a holy empress and a sacred place. Helena had the pagan temple torn down. As the tomb was excavated, the workers found three crosses, along with the sign from Pontius Pilate proclaiming, "This is Jesus of Nazareth, King of the Jews." If you're relic hunting, there's almost no object on earth more important than the True Cross: the cross Christ was crucified on.

But Helena had a problem: there were three crosses, and only one was the True Cross. Undaunted, she brought a woman who was very ill to the tomb and had her touch each of the crosses. The woman touched the first – nothing. She touched the second – still nothing. But when the sick woman touched the third cross, she was immediately healed, and Helena knew which cross to keep safe. Another story says that as the funeral procession of a young man passed, Helena had the crosses held over the man's body. When the shadow of the third cross fell on him, the man returned to life, and the cross was verified.

Helena continued to search for pieces of our Catholic history, eventually finding the nails used at the Crucifixion, the tunic Jesus wore, and even pieces of rope that had been used to tie Him to the cross. Many of these amazing relics are still around today at various monasteries across the world, and we have Helena to thank. Not surprisingly, she's the patron saint of archeologists.

It would have been much simpler, and far more comfortable, for Saint Helena to sit around a palace and live an easy life of privilege, but she did not. How often do you allow yourself to seek comfort over Christ? As Pope Benedict XVI said, "You were not designed for comfort … you were designed for greatness." Ask Saint Helena to pray with you and, through her intercession, for God to open your eyes to the life of adventure and abandon He has designed for you (Ephesians 2:10), to the vocation that only you can fulfill.

Saint Ignatius of Loyola

Feast day: July 31st

Patron of: Jesuit order, Jesuits, retreats, soldiers, and Spiritual Exercises

Many people have heard of the Jesuits, the order of missionary priests who have travelled the world bringing the Gospel to the most remote locations. Far fewer of those people know that a five-foot-two, redheaded soldier from Loyola, Spain named Ignatius, who in his childhood loved himself far more than God or his fellow man, began the Jesuits.

Ignatius of Loyola was the youngest of a dozen children and born into Spanish nobility. He received a military education and entered the army in 1517. After several battles, he was dramatically wounded when a cannonball shattered his shin and left him crippled for life. During his quite lengthy time of recuperation he had little to do but read and was left with only two books – one on saints and one on Christ. Needless to say, he could no longer run from God – spiritually or physically – and the Good Shepherd made his presence known to his sheep, Ignatius.

As his knowledge of Christ grew, so did his humility. Everything changed in Ignatius' exterior life, as his interior, contemplative life was unleashed. He took a vow of chastity, hung up his battle sword, and dressed in a beggar's robes. He left the busyness of the world and retreated to a mountain cave, where he began living what we now know as his "spiritual exercises." When his time as a hermit ended, he travelled as a missionary, sharing the gospel with people of other faiths, including Muslims. At thirty-three he went back to school to study theology and philosophy and was repeatedly imprisoned for his rather "unorthodox" methods of evangelization. Ignatius knew how to make his presence known with love.

Ignatius often received visions in prayer, during which his face was said to shine radiantly; Saint Philip Neri (also found in this book) reported seeing Saint Ignatius' face glow with radiance on frequent occasions. It was not uncommon, either, for him to be seen levitating. The Blessed Virgin Mary herself would often appear to Ignatius, offering direction and predicting events that would happen.

Living out his beliefs so boldly earned Ignatius plenty of enemies in his day. When one such enemy prepared to kill Ignatius with a sword, the man was stopped by a powerful voice that thundered, "What are you doing, you scoundrel?" When another man was angered and took issue with Ignatius, the Lord appeared to him personally, revealing that Saint Ignatius would help be responsible for the salvation of many souls.

Wherever Ignatius went, the power of God went with him. He cured a man of epilepsy and a woman of tuberculosis. He could read the secrets and sins of the people who came to him for counsel. Often when he celebrated Mass, those attending watched as flames appeared and almost "leapt" forth from above his head. He bilocated; witnesses in both Cologne and Rome reported seeing him physically present in both places at once. When he made the sign of the cross, people were instantly healed of sickness and many were cured from demonic possession. A woman with a withered hand was even restored to health simply by washing Saint Ignatius' clothes.

Upon his death in 1556, many who placed flowers beside his casket were healed of various illnesses and diseases; one young girl suffering from tuberculosis was even healed by a piece of his clothing. While his bones were being relocated, many witnessed stars shining in the sky in a sort of "celestial harmony."

Saint Ignatius is a great example of an ordinary guy whom the Lord used to do extraordinary things. He struggled with worldly things but overcame those struggles with heavenly grace. Ignatius of Loyola was a picture of boldness, and he embraced his own personal sufferings and the obstacles of this world with a fierce abandon. His motto of *ad majorem dei gloriam* ("all for the greater glory of God") or "AMDG" became the foundation for the Jesuits, reminding all to live not for our own glory but for the Lord's.

Ask Saint Ignatius of Loyola to pray for you to grow in knowledge, wisdom, and boldness for the gospel. Invite him to pray with you when you're feeling unprepared or too unworthy to preach or teach the truth of the Church. When you're feeling overwhelmed or in a difficult season of your faith journey, remember his words, "If God causes you to suffer much, it is a sign that He has great designs for you, and that He certainly intends to make you a saint." Perhaps one day you'll be known as a saint yourself, or perhaps people will merely see the effects of your saintly life. In either case, regardless of whether earth notices, trust that heaven does.

Saint John Bosco

Feast day: January 31st

Patron of: Christian apprentices, editors, publishers, and schoolchildren

Earlier you read about the story of young Saint Dominic Savio, student of Giovanni "Don" Bosco, a.k.a. Saint John Bosco. To put it in more modern, sci-fi terms: Dominic was the Padawan apprentice and Saint John Bosco, a Jedi Master.

John knew what it was like to have a tough childhood. Born to a poor family of farmers in 1815, he lost his father when he was only two. Though very intelligent and quite witty, John was forced to delay his dreams of priesthood while working as a shepherd and farmer, to help support his mother and siblings. At the age of nine, John Bosco had his first vision, one in which a man with a radiant face and flowing robes called him to lead a group of unruly boys behaving like wild animals. Years later John Bosco would fulfill this prophetic vision, feeling called to the missionary field of youth ministry.

John learned to juggle and to do magic tricks – anything and everything he could think of to catch a child's attention and earn the right to be heard. He served and guided the poor young boys in the city of Turin, many of whom had turned to crime and other sins in order to survive the difficult urban reality into which they were born. John Bosco offered a Catholic education and safe forms of recreation to thousands. He guided them in the ways of the gospel. He cared for them. He fed them. In fact, once when he was saying Mass for 360 young people, there were only eight consecrated hosts left as he began to distribute Communion.

He began to multiply the hosts and, in the end, there was enough for each person present; no one went without Jesus.

Over time, John recruited fellow priests and other friends to help him in his ministry, many of whom left, unable to take any more of the hardships that came with ministering to such a challenging group; two friends even tried to have John Bosco committed to an insane asylum. He was constantly being attacked verbally, physically, and spiritually, but he was not distracted from his mission.

One night while walking home during a particularly rough part of town, two men attacked John. At that very moment a huge, gray dog appeared out of nowhere, pouncing upon the two men and defending the great saint. Assuming the dog was John's, the assailants begged him to call the dog off. Seeing their penitence, John asked the men to promise not to commit crimes again. They agreed as John prayed and the dog relented. When the men ran away, the dog, which John named "Grigio," stayed at his side. From that night forward, Grigio "showed up" whenever John may have been in danger. For almost thirty years, countless eyewitnesses saw the great Mastiff that would mysteriously show up at John's side, becoming something like a crime-fighting sidekick. When asked about the dog's origin and mission, John replied, "It sounds ridiculous to call him an angel, yet he is no ordinary dog."

The saint's life was never boring, to say the least. His visions became more detailed and more miraculous as the years went on. Pope Pius IX even asked John to record his visions, believing them to be prophetic and valuable to the Church. Records of them still exist today and you can read, in detail, the visions and truths the Lord entrusted to this great servant of youth.

Saint John Bosco died in 1888 and his great work is carried on by the Salesians, the order he founded, and also by all who reach out and serve the young Church through youth ministry. He refused to look upon young people the same way that society did, believing that all a young soul needed to live a saintly life was love and truth. If you are a teenager who struggles to believe in your own inherent goodness or an adult struggling with hope for the next generation, ask this great saint to join his prayers to yours. Saint John Bosco saw the good within everyone, which makes it even more fitting that this great saint is one of the famous "incorruptible" saints we hallow today – Saint John Bosco's outside is a perfect reflection of the beauty he possessed on the inside.

Saint John of Beverly

Feast day: October 12th

Patron of: England and the royal household

Have you ever wished you had just the right words to say? Do you have moments where you want to say something, but nothing comes out? Is public speaking scarier to you than meeting some lions in a Roman arena?

If so, you would have loved Saint John of Beverly. He was an English bishop who had a deep love of three things: Christ, contemplation, and caring for the poor. He would often take time to retreat for contemplation, but always made sure to take a poor person with him so that he would have someone to serve while he prayed (think about that the next time your youth group goes on retreat). He ordained a handful of men who later became well known in the Church, including the famous Doctor of the Church, Saint Bede the Venerable. Saint John and Saint Bede were friends, and Bede ended up writing most of the story of John's life and the miracles God performed through him – like when he healed an ill woman with only holy water.

On one retreat, a young man was brought to John whose head was covered with scabs and sores, and who had been mute since birth. After praying over him and applying the remedies he bought for the young man's head, the wounds were healed and a full head of hair grew in their place. Then, on a Sunday, John made the sign of the cross over the youth's tongue and he was able to speak ... but there was one problem. The young man didn't know how – he hadn't learned how to speak because he hadn't been *able* to speak. Patiently, John taught him the alphabet and simple words until the man could communicate fluently.

Even after his death, the people of England loved John of Beverly. In 1415, Henry V won the battle of Agincourt (you Shakespeare fans know what we're talking about) and the king gave John the credit for his victory in the famous battle, almost 700 years after his death in 721.

If your prayer life is usually more talking than listening, Saint John of Beverly might be a saint who you want to put on spiritual speed dial. Contemplative prayer isn't something you just "get good at" but something that requires time, quiet, and effort. Invite Saint John to pray with you when you pray, so that your own prayer life and language would become deeper and more focused on God's will rather than on your own wants. Oh, and be patient with yourself ... Saint John would be. Prayer is less about the words you say and more about the Word – Jesus Christ – speaking to you. You have two ears and one mouth, use them proportionally.

Saint Joseph of Cupertino

Feast day: September 18th

Patron of: air crews, astronauts, aviators, flyers, paratroopers, and students

Saint Joseph of Cupertino's life started off like a scrambled up version of the childhood of Christ. Joseph (the one born in 1603) wasn't a carpenter – but his father was. Sadly, his father died before he was born, and was in so much debt that his mother had to run away and give birth to Joseph in – you guessed it – a stable.

From an early age, Joseph was blessed – and if ever there were a saint who could teach you about the double-edged sword of God's blessings, it'd be Joe. He would have ecstatic visions (think "resting in the Spirit"), but not just in moments of deep prayer. The smallest reminder of God's love – a painting of Christ, a simple prayer, even the sound of church bells – any of them could send him into ecstasy.

That *sounds* great, until you realize that it left Joseph frozen wherever he was standing, mouth open and eyes looking into another part of existence; it actually earned him the nickname "Bocca Aperta" (Open Mouth). And, as you could guess, it's pretty hard to get a steady job if you get a blast of the supernatural every time the church's clock hits the quarter hour. So, after getting harassed by his mom and relatives for being a "do-nothing," he went to the source of all his joy: Christ.

But the adversity didn't stop there for Joe. See, even the religious orders he tried to join wanted him to help out and do work – and as his visions and ecstasies continued to interrupt life, he found himself on the outside looking in yet again. Finally, he found a home with the Franciscans of La Grotella (the little grotto) and was accepted into their community. (If they were cool with Saint Francis talking to birds, a guy having visions couldn't have seemed *that* weird, right?)

You may be thinking to yourself, "Okay, so this guy had a lot of visions – that only seems mildly crazy in comparison to all the other things God's done with saints." But you see, like any good storyteller, we've saved the best for last. Joseph of Cupertino happens to be the patron saint of astronauts and pilots – because he *flew.* Not "LeBron James hovering over people en route to a dunk" flew, but straight-up "hovering above crowds in midair until his superior told him to come down" *flew.*

It happened so much after he joined the Franciscans that he actually had to live in his room for almost thirty-five years, saying Mass and praying in a private chapel away from crowds. When he did go out, he'd come back with his clothes torn up, because people wanted a piece of his robes as a relic (apparently it's true what they say about Catholics always showing up for a free giveaway). One of Joseph's most famous flights was in front of Pope Urban VIII (who didn't start Urban Outfitters, FYI); when Joseph bent down to kiss the Pope's ring, he flew almost thirty feet into the air in front of everyone, and couldn't get down until the head of his order asked him to.

If you find Saint Joseph's story (or any of the stories in this book, for that matter) to be a little "too unbelievable" ask yourself why. Invite Saint Joseph to pray with you and ask the Holy Spirit to open your mind to a realm of new spiritual possibilities. As Scripture reminds us, "All things are possible with God" (Matthew 19:26). The Church celebrates Saint Joseph of Cupertino's feast day on September 18th, but there's no official word from the Vatican on what he did with all those frequent flier miles in heaven.

Saint Lawrence

Feast day: August 10th

Patron of: brewers, butchers, chefs, comedians, cooks, librarians, seminarians, and wine makers

Invoked against: fire and back pain

If there were any saint who'd feel comfortable at an open-mic stand-up comedy night, it would have to be Saint Lawrence. Sure, he was a third century deacon, but the heat of stage lights would have paled in comparison to what he *actually* went through at the end of his life.

Lawrence served as a deacon and treasurer for the early Roman church while they were being persecuted under Valerian (they never seem to run out of emperors who love persecuting Catholics, do they?). There were seven deacons who worked with Pope Saint Sixtus II, and Lawrence guarded the Church's monetary treasure. He was even responsible for keeping safe a great spiritual treasure – the Holy Grail. (If you've never seen an Indiana Jones movie, the Holy Grail is the chalice that Christ used at the Last Supper.)

When the persecution of Catholics really kicked up, Pope Sixtus and six of the deacons were taken to jail for execution. Lawrence, being the only one left behind, asked the Pope why he was leaving without his deacon. Sixtus calmly responded, "In three days you will follow me."

With Pope Sixtus now a martyr along with the six other deacons, Lawrence was the only one left to run the Church. When he was brought before Rome's prefect, it was demanded that he bring all the treasures of the Church to the empire of Rome. Lawrence asked for three days to gather all the riches, and secretly sent the Grail away to be kept safe by his parents. Next, he took every bit of gold or silver the Church had – even the vessels used at Mass – and gave them to poor people around the city.

Then the holy deacon did something both unbelievably beautiful and witty. He gathered all the poor, the sick, and the lame he could find and brought them to the Roman prefect. He presented them as his gift: the riches of the Church.

Every comedian knows that sometimes your audience doesn't like your brand of humor. The prefect was apparently a man without a love for wit, because he sentenced Lawrence to death – a slow and painful death, roasting in a gridiron over a fire. As he slowly died, Lawrence joked with his executioners, asking them to flip him over because he was "done cooking" on one side. Then, three days after the martyrdom of Pope Sixtus II, his ever-faithful deacon joined him in the company of saints. It's interesting – though no surprise – that Saint Lawrence, the patron saint of comedians, would add another funny patronage to his list; he's also the patron saint of tanners (as in, the guys who work with animal hides, not the people who go to tanning salons).

It's easy to lose perspective in life. During particularly difficult weeks or years it can seem like nothing is going your way and everything is terrible. Christ reminded us not to give in to worry or stress (Matthew 6:34) but to be present to God's love and promise in every moment. No matter how bad things get on earth, we are supposed to live for heaven, which is better than our wildest dreams (1 Corinthians 2:9). Ask Saint Lawrence to pray with you and to help you keep a proper and joyful perspective on life.

Saint Margaret of Cortona

Feast day: February 22nd

Patron of: falsely accused people, homeless people, loss of parents, mentally ill people, penitent women, reformed prostitutes, single laywomen, and tertiaries

Invoked against: insanity, mental illness, sexual temptation, and temptations

Few saints' stories would have been more appropriate for a reality show than Margaret of Cortona's. Born in the middle of the thirteenth century, this farmer's daughter's life sounds like a mix between a fairy tale and a Greek tragedy. Margaret was seven when her mother died, and was then forced to live under the care of her father and wicked new stepmother. As a young teenager she was seduced by a nobleman (a knight, to be exact) and ran off with him. Living unashamed as his mistress for over nine years, she bore him a son before one day discovering her lover murdered by thieves.

At that point, everything changed for Margaret. She saw the murder as a sign and immediately repented, publically confessed, and attempted to return to her father's home. He turned his daughter away. Desperate, Margaret took her son and sought refuge with the friars in Cortona. Still young and quite attractive, Margaret gained a lot of attention from men and was constantly battling sexual temptation. In an effort to make herself "less attractive" and show the depth of her penitence, Margaret threatened to cut off her nose and lips. Before she was able to mortify herself into a Picasso painting gone horribly awry, one of the friars persuaded her not to do so.

As the years went on, she tended to the sick and the poor, supporting herself and her son with alms. She became a Franciscan tertiary (third order) in 1277, as her prayer life grew deeper and more intense. She began experiencing "ecstasies," which can be described as a deep, trancelike, mystical state in which the body is overcome with spiritual and physical joy and peace. Far beyond a spiritual high or a temporary, drug-induced state, the saints who experienced ecstasies had powerful out-of-body experiences in which they encountered the love of God in bold, indescribable ways. (The word *ecstasy* comes from the Greek or Latin for "standing outside oneself.")

Once when Margaret was kneeling before the crucifix, Jesus leaned forward and called her "la poverella," which means "the poor one." She and Jesus had frequent conversations over the years; twice our Lord gave her messages for the local bishop, which he ignored ... his stubbornness and pride eventually led to his death. She formed an order of tertiaries like herself and dedicated all of her time to serving the poor, calling her congregation *Poverelle* (Poor Ones).

Margaret developed a strong love of and disciplined prayer for the souls in Purgatory, as well. Apparently, as tradition goes, souls in Purgatory would even appear to Saint Margaret, begging her intercession and prayers on their behalf. As tales of her sordid past came up, Margaret's prayer and devotion to the Eucharist only grew stronger. She became a powerful preacher and, as the years went on, she had a particularly effective ministry reaching out to those who struggled with sexual sins as well as the most hardened sinners of the day; she became known as "the Magdalene of the Franciscans."

This great saint of Cortona prophesied the exact date of her own death and, on her deathbed, became enraptured in her final spiritual ecstasy. She, too, is incorruptible to this day, and millions have visited her resting place and asked for her prayers to God on their behalf.

Though a great sinner in her youth, Saint Margaret of

Though a great sinner in her youth, Saint Margaret of Cortona reminds us all of the power of God's Divine Mercy and the grace of the Sacrament of Reconciliation. Far from perfect, Margaret knew the Perfect One and lived each day to improve. If you or someone you know struggles with sin – especially temptation to sexual sin – or is the victim of gossip or slander because of mistakes made, ask Saint Margaret of Cortona to pray with you. Remember, the only sin God won't forgive is the sin you don't ask forgiveness for. Saint Margaret's story may have begun harshly, but it ends happily ever after ... in heaven.

Saint Martin de Porres

Feast day: November 3rd

Patron of: African-Americans, barbers, social justice, hair stylists, hairdressers, innkeepers, paupers, poor people, and public schools

Invoked against: rats

The lives of the saints are amazing, right? Time and time again we see how God does extraordinary things with humble souls. But one of the "humblest" stories comes from a saint outside the "traditional" saint lists you've probably heard of. He wasn't a rich prince who gave away his wealth or a priest who later became a great bishop. Saint Martin de Porres never even went to Rome; in fact, he never left his hometown of Lima, Peru.

Born in the late sixteenth century, Martin was the illegitimate son of a Spanish knight and a black slave. Thanks to the power of genetics, Martin was dark-skinned; and because of it, his father disowned him for the first eight years of his life. Even though he suffered insults and injustice for being bi-racial, Martin's heart remained set on Christ and a desire to serve. He wanted to be a missionary and martyr, traveling the world to spread God's charity – but God had other plans.

Martin grew up learning a trade as a surgeon's apprentice; when he was a teenager, he brought that skill to the Dominicans (founded by another saint whose story you can also find in this book). Once again, Martin's humility and service were steadfast; he only asked to become a lay brother – part of a group of men and women known as

"Third Order Dominicans" (they still exist today if you want to join!).

As a brother, Martin dedicated himself to helping the poor and sick. His daily goal was to feed one hundred and sixty poor people *every day*! He was known for being able to quickly raise money to give to the poor – something to keep in mind when you need a patron saint for your youth group fundraiser.

Martin was an embodiment of charity and mercy, and the miracles God worked through him were great reflections of his love for the poor. He healed sick people all over Lima, sometimes by giving them something as simple as a glass of water or even – get this – by merely *shaking their hands*. Imagine how grace-filled one of Martin's "high fives" would have been!

As you can guess, medicine wasn't exactly in the same place four hundred years ago as it is now – so when sixty of his brothers got sick, they had to be quarantined in a locked room. Martin knew he needed to minister to them, but couldn't break the quarantine, so he just went through the door. You know, like Jesus did in John 20:19 – *through* the door. When there weren't enough beds in the hospital for the sick, Martin put a sick man in his own bed, and another brother mentioned that Martin might have overdone it. The saintly servant told him it would be "easier to wash sickly sheets than a soul stained with the tears of regret over not helping someone."

Remember when we said that Martin never left Lima? That's true ... kind of. Although he stayed in his hometown all his life, Martin actually appeared to several people (bilocating) on different continents in their times of need. A slave in Africa, a man in Mexico, and many others saw Martin appear. Some even met him again later in Peru – imagine *that* conversation:

"Hey, I saw you in Mexico!"
"I've never been to Mexico."

"Wait, wha'?"

Martin died in 1639, and is still revered around the world as a beautiful example of what happens when humble souls devote themselves to God. When you or your loved ones are ill, invite Saint Martin to be with you and with the doctors, nurses, or caregivers seeking to help. Ask Saint Martin, too, to pray with you to grow in compassion and mercy for all those who are in physical pain and who are suffering from illness. And if God opens doors for you to serve the ill or infirmed, go! Christ didn't just tell us to pray for the sick, He commanded us to visit them (Matthew 25:36).

Saint Martin of Tours

Feast day: November 11th

Patron of: beggars, cavalry, equestrians, reformed alcoholics, and soldiers

Invoked against: alcoholism, impoverishment, and poverty

Catholicism makes use of a lot of military imagery. We talk about spiritual warfare in our prayer lives and about the armor of God in scripture. In our worship, we call God our mighty King and proclaim His victory over evil. Even one of the names for the Church on earth is battle-related: The Church Militant. We have a lot of saints who fought for God, but Saint Martin of Tours is one who truly understood what it means to be a holy soldier.

Raised as a pagan in the third century in Hungary, Martin snuck away from his parents and began going to church with Christians. He was still a catechumen (someone preparing to enter the Church) when he was forced into the cavalry of the Roman Empire. He served in the lands of Gaul, which, even though he didn't know it yet, was God's way of giving him a little sneak preview of his life as a Christian.

As Martin grew in his faith, his time in the cavalry ended up giving him quite a few opportunities to stand for Christ. Before a battle, the young officer announced that he would not fight but, rather, wanted to seek a peaceful resolution; his commanding officers responded by threatening to arrest him. Instead, Martin offered to ride out in front of the army – completely unarmed. Before any fighting could happen, the opposing army asked for peace, and Martin was spared.

It was also during his time as a soldier that Martin experienced one of the greatest miracles of his life. Riding through the forest in the dead of winter, he saw a poor and almost naked man shivering in the cold. Martin got off his horse and used his sword to cut his officer's tunic in half, giving half to the man. Little did Martin know that his attempt to live out Matthew 25:36 was a literal interpretation of the verse, until he had a dream that night. In the dream, he saw Jesus Christ, clothed in half of an officer's cloak and telling his angels, "It was Martin, who is still a catechumen, who clothed me."

Eventually Martin left the army, and started learning the faith under the direction of Saint Hilary. He eventually started a monastery in – you guessed it – Gaul. Martin was asked to become a bishop, but kept saying no until he was tricked into showing up in Tours, where the people of the city begged him to become their shepherd (what a surprise party that must have been!). As bishop, Martin worked tirelessly to defeat heresy and paganism, destroying temples and idols wherever he went. Once, when Martin wanted to cut down a pine tree (because pagans, you know, *worship* trees), the pagans in the town said he could – if he stood in it's way as it fell. Martin complied, and the tree just barely missed him as it hit the ground (that gives whole new meaning to the term "trust fall").

As Martin approached death, his brothers begged him not to leave them. Obedient to the end, he told God that he would stay if it was in the Divine Will. God wanted His holy soldier in heaven, and Saint Martin left Earth in 397. Ask Saint Martin to join his prayers to yours when you pray for those brave men and women in the Armed Forces as well as when you pray that our world leaders might seek and find peaceful resolutions to conflicts. Pray, too, when you are called forth into battle – whether physical or spiritual – that your angels would be with you and the Holy Spirit within you to stand for truth, for peace, and for love, as Christ calls us to do.

Saint Peter of Verona

Feast day: April 29th

Patron of: inquisitors and midwives

Sometimes, the icon (or image) of a saint shows a beautiful story of his or her life. Maybe it's filled with angels, or animals, or other happy things. In the case of Saint Peter of Verona, you really can't say that ... in fact, the word "happy" probably wouldn't come to mind. The first thing you'll normally notice, should you come across a stained glass window or prayer card for Saint Peter of Verona would be an axe – sometimes even an axe stuck in his head. Yes, seriously.

Peter grew up in thirteenth century Italy, with parents who weren't Catholic but still sent him to Catholic school. Little did they know, Peter learned the faith and was converted by the preaching of Saint Dominic himself, who accepted the young man into the Order of Preachers at the age of sixteen. Peter preached to, and converted, many heretics as a young man; but a bold faith can make a lot of enemies, and Peter had them. A group of heretics challenged him to find shade as he spoke to a crowd on a hot day; Peter prayed, and clouds appeared in the sky.

He was visited by saints from heaven, who would converse with him about the glory of God ... which, we're guessing, meant Peter had some pretty solid spiritual direction. But when a passing brother overheard him talking to Saint Catherine, he reported the female voice to his superior. Peter was sent away to live in silent seclusion where there would be no preaching.

Now Peter was upset, understandably. Here he is talking to *saints*, and he's in trouble. He asked God what was going on, and vented his frustration at the injustice of the situation. But you know how God always has the perfect answer? Christ reminded Peter that when He was on earth, He was sinless and put to death on a cross. There's not really a comeback when God reminds you of the Cross, and so Peter learned to grow in love for his suffering.

Luckily, Peter's name was cleared, and he was able to preach to people again. This time, though, his enemies weren't going to let him slide. They hired an assassin to kill him as he traveled, and he was struck in the head with an axe. As he fell to the ground, Peter started to recite the Creed. But simple words were not enough for this martyr to proclaim his faith, so he reached into the wound of his head and used his own blood to begin to write the Creed in the dust. The assassin finished the job by stabbing him in the heart, and then fled.

But killing a saint can have strange consequences, and soon the assassin came before the Dominicans asking for forgiveness. He gave his life to God and became one of the brothers, living a life of virtue until his death.

Many people ask, "Why do bad things happen to good people?" As you can see, Saint Peter wondered the same thing. What people forget, however, is that God is always working for our good and for our salvation (Romans 8:28). The next time you're going through a hard time as a result of living the right kind of life, ask Saint Peter of Verona to pray with you for greater trust and a broader perspective of God's plan. Trust in your beliefs. Trust in the Creed – our foundation of belief that also tells of a good man who suffered greatly … but who also rose in victory!

Saint Philip Neri

Feast day: May 26th

Patron of: joy and the United States

If the Communion of Saints were a deck of cards, Saint Philip Neri would be the Joker. Born in Florence, Italy in 1515, Philip Neri is a saint who knew how to laugh ... at himself. Though he came from a poor family and lost his brother in early childhood, Philip didn't let personal hardship steal his joy. At eighteen years old he arrived in Rome penniless but happy. He tutored to make money, wrote poetry for fun, and began studying philosophy and theology to grow in knowledge. However, Philip wasn't your normal student; he was far more eccentric. When he got tired of learning, he sold all of his books and gave the money to the poor. Philip spent increasingly more time in prayer, fully embracing the life of a hermit.

Philip Neri's prayer life is what kept him so joyful. His entire life became a prayer. He only ate once a day and, even then, it was only bread and water. Though he had a bed, he usually opted to sleep on the floor, without a pillow. He had few possessions, endured great spiritual attacks, and daily, during his intense prayers that lasted hours, it was not uncommon for him to experience ecstasies and visions. During one such night of intense prayer, something miraculous happened to the jolly saint. He felt what is described as a "globe of fiery light" enter his mouth and sink into his heart. He felt great pain in his chest, which over time transformed into pure joy. Witnesses said that the side of Philip's heart was so noticeably swollen that it looked as though there was a fist inside his chest.

In time, Philip wanted to interact with people, so he left his hermit lifestyle; he went out into the city streets and began to preach the gospel, to care for the sick, and to reach out to the poor. A true "do-gooder" in every sense of the word, Philip was funny and charming, and in a short time many people began to work beside him and follow his lead. Philip and his followers built and staffed a hospital with a meeting room where they would gather at night to talk, preach, pray, and listen to music.

At the age of thirty-six, Philip was ordained a priest and his burning heart gave him almost superhuman energy. It's said that some days he'd hear forty confessions before sunrise. He was given the miraculous gift of reading souls, meaning he was able to tell people their sins before they even confessed them. When Philip prayed Mass, witnesses watched in amazement as his face radiated light; occasionally Philip would even levitate during the consecration in a state of ecstasy and sparks would visibly shoot forth from his eyes. In addition to these miraculous displays, it's said that Philip could bilocate and was given the gift of prophecy through his many visions. He once converted a young nobleman by showing him a vision of hell. Philip joked about everything … except sin.

Philip was determined not to let any one of these miraculous "abilities" affect his humility; he never took himself – or anybody else, for that matter – too seriously. Philip liked to keep people on their toes. It was not uncommon to see him walk out into public with his clothes on inside out or with half of his beard shaved off. He loved humor, played practical jokes on his fellow priests, and used unconventional methods to teach people about the love of God.

When Saint Philip died in 1595, an autopsy revealed an abnormally large heart. The spiritual ecstasy and vision that he had was not only proven true but gave miraculous, medical proof to God's glory at work in the saint. If you ever feel like the faith is boring, if you've lost your joy, or if you worry that you can't be holy *and have fun* in this life, ask Saint Philip Neri, God's joker, to pray with you. The only reason to take this life too seriously is if it's your only one! Heaven awaits and Saint Philip is there waiting for you ... bless his heart!

Saint Pio

Feast day: September 23rd

Patron of: the unborn, confessors, Catholic adolescents, and civil defense volunteers

There are countless words we could use to describe Saint (Padre) Pio of Pietrelcina, but the simplest way to put it might be this: Saint Pio is like the Communion of Saints' Navy SEAL. To be listed in the Communion of Saints is a great honor, to be sure, but even among that list, Pio tends to stand out for many reasons. Keep reading and you'll see why...

While most of the saints we've been talking about in this book died hundreds of years ago, Pio died in 1968. He was canonized by (future saint) Blessed John Paul II in 2002. Born in 1887 in Pietrelcina, Italy, this amazing saint was ordained at the age of twenty-two and survived both World Wars, immense personal sufferings, and also some of the worst spiritual attacks ever recorded by saintly biographers.

In 1918, while praying before a crucifix, Pio received the stigmata (the wounds of Christ), which he bore for fifty years. The pain from the wounds was great, and the pain was intensified during the Thursday and Friday of Holy Week each year. When Pio was asked if the stigmata hurt, he replied, "Do you think the Good Lord gave them to me just for decoration?" Once, when a hernia had rendered Pio unconscious and in need of surgery, the doctor preparing for the operation looked at the saint's left side where one of the (stigmata) wounds of Christ was located. The doctor reported that the wound was fresh and in the shape of a cross, with rays of light pouring forth from it.

Pio had the miraculous ability to bilocate as well. Apparently, during World War II, Pio appeared in front of an aircraft preparing to bomb his village and thus his town was spared from destruction. There was another report of Pio bilocating to warn troops in the battlefield of dangers, saving several from certain death, and there were countless encounters that people had with the great saint in various cities around the world; meanwhile, Pio never left his cell in the monastery. In one instance, a man sent Pio a telegram asking him to pray for his mother-in-law who had a deadly tumor. Almost immediately, a mysterious friar appeared in the room of the woman with the tumor – although no one had let the friar in. He blessed her and disappeared; days later an exam revealed that the tumor was gone. Hundreds more stories like this one exist and are all traced back to the same friar, Pio of Pietrelcina.

In the modern twentieth century, word spread quickly about this holy man of God. Everyone wanted to see him and to touch him in hopes of a miraculous healing. Luckily, Pio also had the gift of levitation, which came in handy when he needed to get through a swarm of people all eager to grab him or, at the very least, rip off a piece of his robe. Pio had achieved "rock star" status although he never wanted it. One day he was forced to levitate through the air just to reach the confessional. Pio was a Sacramental force to be reckoned with, hearing confessions from sun up to sun down. Like some others in this book, he had the ability to read peoples' souls, too.

The list of Pio's miraculous feats is long and incredible. He raised a boy from the dead. He restored a young girl's sight simply by making the Sign of the Cross upon her eyes. He had a holy odor, far more pungent than any cologn;, when Pio was praying for someone, the person would apparently smell roses and incense – even if the person was hundreds of miles away! Can you imagine that? More personal than any text message, more powerful than Skype!

Beyond all the hype that surrounded him, Pio remained humble. He served the poor and suffering with

humble. He served the poor and suffering with uncondi-
tional love and reckless abandon. When his fame threatened
to detract from the ministry at hand, he celebrated Mass in
private, and when asked not to preach publically, he embraced the directive with strict and joyful obedience. Upon
Pio's death the stigmata wounds disappeared ... and they
left no scar.

If you are suffering physically, emotionally, mentally, or
spiritually, Pio is a powerful intercessor. He knew well the
physical challenges and spiritual obstacles that come with
living a holy life. You are not alone! In the saints, God gives
us the tremendous gift of brothers and sisters in the faith
who live (in heaven) to pray for us. Specifically ask Saint Pio
to pray with you and for you and trust that with God's grace
you, like Pio, can bear any cross that comes your way.

Saint Rita of Cascia

Feast day: May 22nd

Patron of: abuse victims, difficult marriages, parenthood, and widows

Invoked against: infertility, loneliness, sickness, sterility, and wounds

Some saint stories almost seem made for a big-budget summer blockbuster film, utilizing the most state-of-the-art special effects to bring their miraculous feats and inexplicable lives "to life" on the big screen.

Then, there are saints like Saint Rita of Cascia, whose story seems more fitting for a heart-wrenching, tear-jerking television soap opera or cable mini-series. Saint Rita was born to elderly parents in Cascia, Italy, late in the fourteenth century. At the age of twelve, Rita was betrothed to marry a horrible man – a local gangster named Paolo who had an adulterous heart and a terrible temper. Rita obeyed her parents and, at eighteen, married him. Over the next eighteen years, Saint Rita bore twin sons – which brought her the only joy outside of God, as she was both neglected and abused by her drunken, constantly cheating husband. Eventually, Paolo was killed by some of his enemies; but when the sons wanted to avenge their father's death, it was their mother's prayers that converted their hearts.

Rita's sons then became ill and died soon after. Now alone at age thirty-six, Rita went to the local Augustinian monastery in hopes of joining the nuns there. Initially, she was denied entrance since she was not a virgin; but, one night, Rita was miraculously delivered into their midst (into a cloistered convent, behind locked doors), and they were so astounded by the miracle that they had no choice but to let her in.

For the next forty years, Rita lived and worked within her religious community, serving all she encountered and working for peace in her violent region of Italy. It was during this time that Rita received a miraculous sign of Christ's love, for which she became widely known (even to this day).

Saint Rita used to actually pray to suffer as Christ did; so strong was her devotion to Christ's Passion that it's reported that while she was praying, Christ (in His mercy) consented to her request and sent a thorn from His crown flying across the room to be lodged in her forehead. It was noticeable to all, causing her chronic headaches, noticeable bleeding, and even a foul stench that no one could miss. This "blessing" went on for fifteen years, causing many to grow in their devotion to the Lord and in gratitude for His Passion. Undoubtedly, there has never been a holier headache in history.

The saint's suffering did not stop there, either. She spent the final four years of her life bedridden as her health worsened. Rita did not eat much more than the Eucharist daily, yet she had enough strength to teach, direct, and counsel the younger sisters who spent time at her bedside.

It's said that in her final days a visitor from her hometown asked her if there was anything she wanted; Rita's last request was for a single rose to be brought to her from her family's estate. Though it was January and the request was seen as impossible in the dead of winter, the visitor arrived to find an otherwise barren and dead rose bush with one single rose in blossom. After her death, the foul stench that previously accompanied her wound became a beautiful odor – one that still permeates the convent in which she lived over 500 years ago. In fact, you can see Rita's incorrupt body on display in that same convent. Her life stands as a hope-filled witness to all of us – most especially the abused, the sick, those in difficult marriages, and those suffering great physical pain; all for whom she is a patroness and intercessor.

Saint Rita reminds us to be careful about what you pray for and that God is faithful to the end ... and then some. Invite Saint Rita into your prayer each and every time you begin to think that God is testing or trying you beyond what you can bear. Pray, too, that you can look upon the trials of life as gifts from the Lord (James 1:2) – signs that He believes you're faithful and wants you to grow in virtue, to help you become a saint.

Saint Teresa of Avila

Feast day: October 15th

Patron of: Headache sufferers, Catholic writers, and people in religious orders

If you heard a teenage guy describing a girl as "witty and beautiful, intelligent and charming, funny and deep," you might assume he was talking about his dream girl, but he could have easily been describing young Teresa of Avila, Spain. Born in 1515, Teresa entered a world embroiled in change. Columbus had just introduced Europe to the new world. Martin Luther's issues with the Church were about to explode into what we now call the Reformation. There was a battle going on between those people seeking God and those seeking only the *comforts* that came with "seeking" God. In fact, Teresa's own life reflected this tension.

You could say that Teresa was the average teen, but not the average "saint." She developed a love for clothes and perfume … and boys. An interior battle erupted within Teresa, between loving created things more than their Creator. The holy girl also wanted to be a girly girl. She cared about fashion and looking cute and flirting far more than her overprotective father was comfortable with or willing to allow. Finally, her father became so enraged by his wild child's antics that he sent Teresa to live in a Carmelite convent when she turned sixteen; but her life in the convent only added to her struggle.

Many of the convents at the time had become more about pursuing the world than heaven. The women were allowed to do their hair, wear jewelry, and don attractive veils and other beautiful garments that in no way could be considered modest or simple. Young men were even allowed to visit the ladies at Teresa's convent. All of these worldly luxuries – combined with Teresa's natural charm and beauty – ensured her a long line of male suitors and female gossipers, but did little to ease her love for created things.

Teresa contracted malaria, which later led to three years of paralysis. Her physical suffering became unbearable; but rather than pray *more*, Teresa actually prayed less (and considering the fact that she's now a saint, this should make us feel less guilty about our own spiritual dry spells). She struggled with prayer, blamed her sickness on her own sinfulness, and proclaimed that she didn't deserve God's love or mercy. She would literally count the minutes during her holy hour, waiting impatiently for it to be over. This woman hardly seemed like the person who would later be known to millions as "Teresa of the Child Jesus."

Finally though, at the age of 41, a priest convinced Teresa to really start praying again. Teresa prayed, and boy, did God listen (as He promises us in Jeremiah 29:12). Teresa began receiving visions and gifts from God in prayer, often finding herself in a state of ecstasy and frequently levitating. The visions often caused her intense mental and physical distress; once, during an ecstasy, Teresa described her experience of God's love "like a lance driven into her heart." Her sufferings brought with them an intense intimacy with God and also an authenticity that few other saints have expressed so freely. During a particularly difficult time Teresa exclaimed, "God if this is how you treat your friends it's no wonder you have so few!"

The spiritual gifts far outweighed her physical pains, however, bringing Teresa peace, encouragement, and a clear goal. Unlike Martin Luther who tried to reform the Church from the outside, Teresa would obediently and humbly work for change from within the Church. She founded a new convent for Carmelite sisters that was devoted to a life of poverty and intense prayer. Teresa founded seventeen convents before her death and restored order to the ... um, order. Both nuns and priests were (and still are) inspired by

Teresa's holy example of simplicity and prayerfulness.

The pursuit of holiness became the goal of Teresa's life and writings. It's even said that Teresa would "glow" with light at different times. Her works – including *The Interior Castle*, a mystical, literary classic – are some of the finest writings about the interior spiritual life, and have helped earn her the title "Doctor of the Church."

Years after being exhumed from the grave, Teresa's body – completely incorrupt –emitted a sweet-smelling, almost "heavenly" fragrance (which is ironic, given her childhood fascination with perfume). Her incorrupt body resides in Avila, and her heart is displayed separately under glass– revealing a deep wound within it as Teresa had mystically explained in her aforementioned vision – for all to see and venerate.

Whenever you find yourself caught in the tug-of-war be-tween heaven and earth, in the epic battle between your flesh and your spirit, ask Saint Teresa of Avila to pray with you. Over time, she learned what it meant to be in the world but not of it. And if you ever doubt whether God is listening to your prayers or, in your sufferings, fear that God may be punishing you for all the sins you've committed, ask Saint Teresa to take you by the hand and walk you to the Cross. Her intercession will help remind you that no matter how difficult or painful your life can become at times, the Lord's mercy is always greater than your sin and His love far deeper than you can imagine.

Conclusion

Okay, you've read these amazing stories of the saints, but now what? What impact will these incredible stories of heroic lives have on *your* life? It's not enough just to say, "Wow, that story was insane!" or "I still can't believe that happened." The stories of the saints are important not only for us to know but also to share. These saints are our brothers and sisters in Christ. The Communion of Saints are a part of our family – their lives tell us about the history of the Church and the Catholic faith while simultaneously inspiring us to *keep moving forward*, all the way to Heaven.

You might not know very much about this saintly family tree, but you should. It's incredible. Our family has a long legacy. Our family has made a huge impact on the world. In fact, our family has changed the world in almost every conceivable way. If it weren't for our family, modern culture would look a whole lot different and far darker than it does.

Our Catholic family tree has born a lot of fruit, my brothers and sisters, and it's fruit that has remained (John 15:16).

Do you set up a Nativity set at your house during Advent? That was **Saint Francis of Assisi**'s idea first.

The Christmas tree? Many credit that tradition's "roots" (or lack thereof) to **Saint Boniface**. Incidentally, he also gets credited with inventing what we now call "bowling." **Saint Nicholas** gave us far more than stockings or a Christmas icon ... as an early Bishop, it was his charity in the face of early Christian persecution that pointed pagan souls back to Christ.

Do you go to Catholic school? You can thank **Saint Elizabeth Ann Seton** for those. Perhaps you're in college at a state school and go to a Newman center for Mass? You can thank **Blessed Cardinal Newman**. In fact, many would credit **Saint Bonaventure** and **Saint Thomas Aquinas** for their roles in the creation of international universities, beginning back in Salamanca. If you end up in law school, you might want to give a shout out to **Saint Thomas More**, whose own comprehension of the legal system and unwavering approach to truth later influenced the writings of John Locke.

Oh, and if you're called to the discern the priesthood, you should be sure to give a shout out to **Saint Charles Borromeo**, since he was so instrumental in creating the modern seminary system.

I'll bet if you look around your local community, you'll even find a local chapter of the Society of **Saint Vincent de Paul**, specializing in outreach to the poor. His legacy of charity is alive and strong over 450 years after his death.

Some saints were so holy that they were honored far more after they died. **Saint Gregory the Great** didn't create Gregorian chant, but due to his legacy it was named after him, as was the Gregorian calendar. It's reported that **Saint Therese of Lisieux** had the academic equivalence of a sixth grader, but her holiness and practical insights into Christian love later earned her the esteemed title "Doctor of the Church" (a title that's only been given to 34 saints).

Saint Benedict created the modern monastic community, blessing and housing hundreds of thousands of holy men and women who have served the Church. **Saint Ignatius of Loyola** gave the Church and the world a new understanding and vision of the Church's missionary work. **Saint Dominic** radically changed the concept of religious life among the laity. **Saint Augustine** came up with a rule of life still followed by Diocesan priests.

A huge number of the capitals and major cities in our country were founded by Catholic religious orders. St. Louis, St. Paul, and St. Petersburg all began as Mission Churches.

Most of the major cities in California are named after saints, thanks to **Blessed Junipero Serra**. In fact, the full name of Los Angeles is actually *El Pueblo de la Reina de Los Angeles* (The Town of the Queen of the Angels). Los Angeles is named after Our Lady.

Blessed (Mother) Theresa of Calcutta began the Missionaries of Charity and changed the way the world perceives human dignity. Blessed **John Paul II** (John Paul the Great) gave us far more than the Theology of the Body or the New Evangelization. World Youth Days have become the largest gatherings in the history of the civilized world. Pope John Paul II's works and words on existential phenomenology and his work to bring down the Communist regime in Eastern Europe will never be forgotten.

Oh, and last but far from least, you know that Bible of yours? The Catholic Church put that together into its final form. Catholic Church fathers prayerfully deliberated, debated, and discerned which books would "make the cut" (into what's known as the *canon*). **Saint Jerome**, too, played a critical role in the Bible's translation into Latin, insuring its timelessness and universality (and let's not forget that Catholic means "universal").

What is even more enduring than the saints' earthly legacies, however, is their legacy of love. They are saints not because of impressive resumes; they are saints because they held nothing back. They are saints because they served God and His people with their whole hearts. That is the legacy we should truly celebrate. Everything they did in God's name would be empty without their love for Him (1 Corinthians 13:1-3), but because of their focus on the Lord, we can look back now with great pride in our family tree and see all that the Lord achieved through a series of willing sinners ... just like us.

It's good to be Catholic.

DOCTORS OF THE CHURCH

January 2
- St. Basil

January 2
- St. Gregory Nazianzus

January 13
- St. Hilary of Poitiers

January 24
- St. Francis de Sales

January 28
- St. Thomas Aquinas

February 21
- St. Peter Damian

March 18
- St. Cyril of Jerusalem

April 4
- St. Isidore

April 21
- St. Anselm

April 29
- St. Catherine of Siena

May 2
- St. Athanasius

May 25
- St. Bede, the Venerable

June 9
- St. Ephraem of Syria

June 13
- St. Anthony of Padua

June 27
- St. Cyril of Alexandria

July 15
- St. Bonaventure

July 21
- St. Lawrence of Brindisi

July 30
- St. Peter Chrysologus

August 1
- St. Alphonsus Liguori

August 20
- St. Bernard of Clairvaux

August 28 - St. Augustine

September 3
- St. Gregory the Great

September 13
- St. John Chrysostom

September 17
- St. Robert Bellarmine

September 30
- St. Jerome

October 1
- St. Therese of Lisieux

October 15
- St. Teresa of Avila

November 10
- St. Leo the Great

December 14
– St. John of Avila

November 15
- St. Albert

December 4
- St. John Damascene

December 7
- St. Ambrose

December 14
- St. John of the Cross

December 21
- St. Peter Canisius

PATRON SAINT
INDEX

Abuse victims
- Adelaide
- Agostina Pietrantoni
- Fabiola
- Germaine Cousin
- Godelieve
- Jeanne de Lestonnac
- Jeanne Marie de Maille
- Joaquina Vedruna de Mas
- Laura Vicuna
- Margaret the Barefooted
- Maria Bagnesi
- Monica
- Pharaildis
- Rita of Cascia

Academics
- Brigid of Ireland
- Catherine of Alexandria
- Nicholas of Myra
- Thomas Aquinas

Accountants
- Matthew the Apostle

Accused people, falsely
- Blandina
- Dominic de Guzman
- Dominic Savio
- Elizabeth of Hungary
- Elizabeth of Portugal
- Gerard Majella

- Helen of Skofde
- Margaret of Antioch
- Margaret of Cortona
- Marinus
- Matilda
- Menas
- Philip Howard
- Raymond Nonnatus
- Roch
- Serenus

Actors
- Genesius
- Vitus

Actresses
- Pelagia

Adopted children
- Clotilde
- Thomas More
- William of Rochester

Advertisers, advertising
- Bernadine of Siena

Against abortions
- Catherine of Sweden

Against battle
- Florian

Against bad weather
- Eurosia
- Medard

Against inflammatory diseases
- Benedict

Against perjury
- Felix of Nola
- Pancras

Against sorcery, witchcraft
- Benedict
- Columba of Rieti

Against throats ailments
- Andrew the Apostle
- Blaise
- Etheldreda
- Godelieve
- Ignatius of Antioch
- Lucy of Syracuse
- Swithbert

AIDS patients
- Aloysius Gonzaga
- Peregrine Laziosi
- Therese of Lisieux

Alcoholism
- John of God
- Martin of Tours
- Matthias the Apostle
- Monica
- Urban of Langres

Arm pain; pain in the arms
- Amalburga

Armies
- Maurice

Art
- Catherine of Bologna

Athletes
- Sebastian

Automobile drivers
- Christopher
- Elijah the Prophet
- Frances of Rome
- Sebastian of Aparicio

Bachelors
- Benedict Joseph Labre
- Benezet
- Boniface of Tarsus
- Caesarius of Nanzianzen
- Casimir of Poland
- Christopher
- Cuthman
- Epipodius
- Gerald of Aurillac
- Guy of Anderlecht
- John Rigby
- Joseph Moscati
- Luke the Apostle
- Marinus
- Pantaleon
- Roch
- Serenus
- Theobald

Baptism
- John the Baptist

Bodily ills, sickness
- Alphais
- Alphonsa of India
- Angela Merici
- Angela Truszkowska
- Arthelais
- Bathild
- Bernadette of Lourdes
- Camillus of Lellis
- Catherine del Ricci
- Catherine of Siena
- Drogo

- Edel Quinn
- Elizabeth of the Trinity
- Gerard of Villamagna
- Germaine Cousin
- Gorgonia
- Hugh of Lincoln
- Isabella of France
- Jacinta Marto
- John of God
- Julia Billiart
- Julia Falconieri
- Juliana of Nicomedia
- Louis IX
- Louise de Marillac
- Lydwina of Schiedam
- Maria Bagnesi
- Maria Gabriella
- Maria Mazzarello
- Marie Rose Durocher
- Mary Ann de Paredes
- Mary Magdalen of Pazzi
- Michael the Archangel
- Our Lady of Lourdes
- Paula Frassinetti
- Peregrine Laziosi
- Philomena
- Rafka Al-Rayes
- Raphael the Archangel
- Romula
- Syncletica
- Teresa of Avila
- Teresa Valse Pantellini
- Terese of the Andes
- Therese of Lisieux

Bowel disorder
- Bonaventure

Boy Scouts
- Amand
- George

Breast disease, invoked against
- Agatha

Brides
- Adelaide
- Blaesilla
- Catherine of Genoa
- Clotilde
- Delphina
- Dorothy of Caesarea
- Dorothy of Montau
- Elizabeth of Hungary
- Elizabeth of Portugal
- Hedwig
- Ida of Herzfeld
- Ivetta of Huy
- Margaret the Barefooted
- Nicholas of Myra

Broadcasters
- Gabriel the Archangel

Broken bones
- Drogo
- Stanislaus Kostka

Cancer patients
- Aldegundis
- Ezekiel Moreno
- Giles
- James Salomone
- Peregrine Laziosi

Catechists
- Cesar de Bus
- Charles Borromeo
- Robert Bellarmine
- Viator

Catechumens
- Charles Borromeo
- Robert Bellarmine

Charities, charitable workers
- Elizabeth of Hungary
- Elizabeth of Portugal
- Vincent de Paul

Chastity, invoked for
- Agnes of Rome
- Thomas Aquinas

Child abuse victims
- Alodia
- Germaine Cousin
- Lufthild
- Nunilo

Children whose parents were not married
- Brigid of Ireland
- Eustochium of Padua
- Sibyllina Biscossi

Colleges, schools, universities
- Contardo Ferrini
- Infant Jesus of Prague
- Joseph Calasanz
- Thomas Aquinas

Comedians, comediennes
- Genesius
- Lawrence
- Vitus

Computers, computer technicians
- Isidore of Seville

Confessions, to make a
good one
- Gerard Majella
- John Nepomucene

Cyclists
- La Madonna di Ghisalo

Dancers
- Genesius
- Philemon
- Vitus

Deaf people
- Cadoc of Llancarvan
- Drogo
- Francis de Sales
- Meriadoc
- Ouen

Demonic possessed people
- Amabilis
- Bruno
- Cyriacus
- Denis
- Dymphna
- Dionysius the Aeropagite
- Lucian
- Lucy Bufalari
- Marcian
- Margaret of Fontana
- Quirinus
- Ubaldus Baldassini

Desperate, forgotten, im-
possible or lost causes or
situations
- Jude Thaddeus
- Gregory Thaumaturgus
- Philomena
- Rita of Cascia

Difficult marriages
- Castora Gabrielli
- Catherine of Genoa
- Dorothy of Montau
- Edward the Confessor
- Elizabeth of Portugal
- Fabiola
- Gengulphus
- Godelieve
- Gummarus
- Hedwig
- Helena
- Louis IX
- Margaret the Barefooted
- Marguerite d'Youville
- Monica
- Nicholas of Flue
- Olaf II
- Pharaildis
- Philip Howard
- Radegunde
- Rita of Cascia
- Theodore of Sykeon
- Thomas More
- Wilgefortis
- Zedislava Berka

Difficult situations
- Eustachius

Disabled or physically
challenged
people
- Alphais
- Angela Merici
- Gerard of Aurillac
- Germaine Cousin
- Giles
- Henry II
- Lutgardis
- Margaret of Castello

- Seraphina
- Servatus
- Servulus

Doubt
- Joseph
- Thomas the Apostle

Drug addiction
- Maximillian Kolbe

Dying alone; against solitary
death
- Francis of Assisi

Dysfunctional families
- Eugene de Mazenod

Earaches
- Cornelius
- Polycarp of Smyrna

Elderly people
- Anthony of Padua

Engaged couples
- Ambrose Sansedoni of
  Siena
- Valentine

Ecologists,
environmentalism
- Francis of Assisi
- Kateri Tekakwitha

Equestrians
- Anne
- George
- James the Greater
- Martin of Tours

Faith in the Blessed
Sacrament
- Anthony of Padua

Fainting, faintness
- Urban of Langres
- Ursus of Ravenna
- Valentine

Families
- Adalbald of Ostrevant
- Adelaide
- Clotilde
- Dagobert II
- Dorothy of Montau
- Edwin
- Ferdinand III of Castille
- Ivetta of Huy
- Leonidas
- Leopold
- Louis IX
- Margaret of Scotland
- Matilda
- Nicholas of Flue
- Richard Gwyn
- Thomas More
- Vladimir

Fathers
- Joachim
- Joseph

Firefighters
- Barbara
- Catherine of Siena
- Eustachius
- Florian
- John of God

For help with conception
- Agatha
- Anne
- Anthony of Padua
- Casilda of Toledo
- Felicity
- Fiacre
- Francis of Paola
- Giles
- Henry II
- Margaret of Antioch
- Medard
- Philomena
- Rita of Cascia
- Theobald Roggeri

For people with mental illness, mental handicaps, and, against depression
- Amabilis
- Benedict Joseph Labre
- Bibiana
- Christina the Astonishing
- Drogo
- Dymphna
- Eustochium of Padua
- Fillan
- Giles
- Job
- Margaret of Cortona
- Maria Fortunata Viti
- Medard
- Michelina
- Osmund
- Raphaela
- Romanus of Condat
- Veran

Freedom
- Infant Jesus of Prague

Friendships
- John the Apostle

Gambling addiction
- Bernadine of Siena

Girl Scouts
- Agnes of Rome

Governors, rulers, authorities
- Ferdinand III of Castile

Grandparents
- Anne
- Joachim

Grooms
- Louis IX
- Nicholas of Myra

Guardian angels
- Raphael the Archangel

Happy marriages
- Valentine

Head injuries
- John Licci

Headaches
- Acacius
- Anastasius the Persian
- Bibiana
- Denis
- Dionysius the Aeropagite
- Gerard of Lunel
- Gereon
- Pancras
- Stephen the Martyr
- Teresa of Avila

- William Firmatus

Health
- Infant Jesus of Prague

Hemorraghes
- Lucy of Syracuse

Homeless people
- Benedict Joseph Labre
- Edwin
- Elizabeth of Hungary
- Lufthild
- Margaret of Corton

Homemakers, housewives
- Anne
- Martha
- Monica
- Zita

In-law problems
- Adelaide
- Elizabeth of Hungary
- Elizabeth Ann Seton
- Godelieve
- Helen of Skofde
- Jeanne de Chantal
- Jeanne Marie de Maille
- Ludmila
- Marguerite d'Youville
- Michelina
- Pulcheria

Incest victims
- Dymphna
- Laura Vicuna
- Winifred of Wales

Internet
- Isidore of Seville

Jealousy
- Elizabeth of Portugal

Journalists, news staff
- Francis de Sales
- Maximillian Kolbe
- Paul the Apostle

Knowledge
- Holy Spirit

Laborers
- Eligius
- Guy of Anderlecht
- Isidore the Farmer
- James the Greater
- John Bosco
- Joseph
- Lucy

Lay people, laity
- Frances of Rome
- Paul the Apostle

Learning
- Acca
- Ambrose of Milan
- Margaret of Scotland
- Nicholas Albergati
- Thomas Aquinas

Lectors
- Bede the Venerable
- Pollio
- Sabas

Liberal arts
- Catherine of Bologna

Loneliness
- Rita of Cascia

Longevity, long life
- Peter the Apostle

Loss of parents, mother, father
- Alphonsa of India
- Angela Merici
- Colette
- Dymphna
- Elizabeth of the Trinity
- Elizabeth Ann Seton
- Gemma Galgani
- Germaine Cousin
- Humbeline
- Jeanne de Chantal
- Jeanne Marie de Maille
- Kateri Tekawitha
- Laura Vicuna
- Louise de Marillac
- Margaret of Cortona
- Margaret Mary Alacoque
- Marguerite Bourgeous
- Marguerite d'Youville
- Maria Bagnesi
- Maria Fortunata Viti
- Maria Gabriella
- Maria Goretti
- Mariana of Quito
- Marie of the Incarnation
- Marie Rose Durocher
- Pulcheria
- Radegunde
- Rafka Al-Rayes
- Sibyllina Biscossi
- Syncletica
- Teresa of Avila
- Teresa Benedicta
- Therese of Lisieux

Lost keys, against losing keys
- Zita

Love
- Dwynwen
- Raphael the Archangel
- Valentine

Married couples
- Joseph

Mechanics
- Catherine of Alexandria

Migraine; against migraines; migraine sufferers
- Gereon
- Severus of Avranches
- Ubaldus Baldassini

Miscarriages
- Catherine of Siena
- Catherine of Sweden

Missionaries
- Francis Xavier
- Therese of Lisieux

Mothers
- Anne
- Gerard Majella
- Monica

Motherhood
- John Berchmans
- John Bosco
- Maria Goretti
- Pedro Calungsod
- Philomena
- Raphael the Archangel

Mountain climbers
- Bernard of Menthon

Musicians
- Benedict Biscop
- Cecilia
- Dunstan
- Genesius of Rome
- Gregory the Great
- Notkar Balbulus
- Paul the Apostle

Naval officers
- Francis of Paola

Newborn babies, infants
- Brigid of Ireland
- Holy Innocents
- Nicholas of Tolentino
- Philip of Zell
- Philomena
- Raymond Nonnatus
- Zeno of Verona

Newlyweds
- Dorothy of Caesarea
- Nicholas of Myra
  Nightmares
- Raphael the Archangel

Nuns
- Ada
- Blessed Virgin Mary
- Brigid of Ireland
- Gertrude the Great
- Scholastica

Nurses
- Agatha
- Alexius
- Camillus of Lellis

- Catherine of Alexandria
- Catherine of Siena
- John of God
- Margaret of Antioch
- Raphael the Archangel

Newborn babies, infants
- Brigid of Ireland
- Holy Innocents
- Nicholas of Tolentino
- Philip of Zell
- Philomena
- Raymond Nonnatus
- Zeno of Verona

Obsession
- Quirinus

Opposition from Church
authorities
- Elizabeth Ann Seton
- Joan of Arc
- Marguerite d'Youville
- Mary MacKillop
- Mary Magdalena
  Bentivoglio
- Rose Philippine Duchesne
- Teresa of Avila

Oversleeping
- Vitus

Pain, pain relief
- Madron

Parenthood
- Adelaide
- Clotilde
- Ferdinand III of Castille
- Louis IX
- Rita of Cascia

Peace
- Barnabas
- Elizabeth of Portugal
- Francis of Assisi
- Infant Jesus of Prague
- Irene
- Norbert

Penitent sinners
- Mary Magdalen

People
- Mary, Mother of God

Physicians
- Cosmas
- Damian
- Luke the Apostle
- Pantaleon
- Raphael the Archangel

Pilots
- Joseph of Cupertino
- Our Lady of Loreto
- Therese of Lisieux

Poets
- Brigid of Ireland
- Cecilia
- Columba
- David

Police officers
- Michael the Archangel
- Sebastian

Poor people
- Anthony of Padua
- Ferdinand III of Castille
- Giles
- Lawrence

- Martin de Porres
- Nicholas of Myra
- Philomena
- Zoticus of Constantinople

Prisoners of war, pow's
- Leonard of Noblac
- Walter of Pontnoise

Priests
- John Mary Vianney
- Philomena

Pro-life movement
- Gerard Majella
- Maximillian Kolbe

Procrastination
- Expeditus

Prolonged suffering
- Lydwina of Schiedam

Radio
- Gabriel the Archangel

Rape victims
- Agatha
- Agnes of Rome
- Antonia Messina
- Dymphna
- Joan of Arc
- Maria Goretti
- Pierina Morosini
- Potamiaena
- Solange
- Zita

Retreats
- Ignatius of Loyola

Seminarians
- Charles Borromeo
- Lawrence

Separated spouses
- Edward the Confessor
- Gengulphus
- Gummarus
- Nicholas of Flue
- Philip Howard

Sexual temptation
- Angela of Foligno
- Catherine of Siena
- Margaret of Cortona
- Mary of Edessa
- Mary of Egypt
- Mary Magdalen
- Mary Magdalen of Pazzi
- Pelagia of Antioch

Silence
- John Nepomucene

Singers; vocalists
- Andrew the Apostle
- Cecilia
- Gregory the Great

Single laywomen
- Agatha
- Alodia
- Bibiana
- Emiliana
- Flora of Cordoba
- Gudule
- Julitta
- Margaret of Cortona
- Martha
- Nunilo
- Praxides

- Syncletica
- Tarsilla
- Zita

Skaters
- Lydwina of Schiedam

Skiers
- Bernard of Menthon

Slander
- John Nepomucene

Souls in purgatory
- Nicholas of Tolentino
- Odilo

Spasms
- John the Baptist

Speakers, lecturers
- John Chrysostom
- Justin Martyr

Spousal abuse; (physical)
- Rita of Cascia

Spousal abuse; (verbal)
- Anne Marie Taigi
- Godelieve
- Monica

Starving people
- Anthony of Padua

Storms, against
thunderstorms
- Agrippina
- Barbara
- Catald
- Christopher

- Erasmus
- Florian
- Gratus of Aosta
- Henry of Upsalla
- Hermengild
- Jodocus
- Our Lady of Zapopan
- Scholastica
- Thomas Aquinas
- Urban of Langres
- Vitus
- Walburga

Students
- Albertus Magnus
- Ambrose of Milan
- Benedict
- Catherine of Alexandria
- Gabriel of the Sorrowful
  Mother
- Gregory the Great
- Isidore of Seville
- Jerome
- John Bosco
- Joseph Calasanz
- Joseph of Cupertino
- Lawrence
- Nicholas of Myra
- Osanna Andreasi
- Symphorian of Autun
- Thomas Aquinas
- Ursula

Swimmers, swimming
- Adjutor

Teachers, educators
- Catherine of Alexandria
- Francis de Sales
- Gregory the Great
- John Baptist de La Salle

- Ursula

Teenagers
- Aloyisius Gonzaga

Telephones
- Clare of Assisi
- Gabriel the Archangel

Television
- Clare of Assisi
- Gabriel the Archangel
- Martin de Porres

Temptations
- Angela of Foligno
- Benedict
- Catherine of Bologna
- Catherine of Genoa
- Catherine of Siena
- Columba of Rieti
- Cyriacus
- Elizabeth of Schonau
- Eustochium of Padua
- Gemma Galgani
- Helen del Cavalcanti
- Margaret of Cortona
- Maria Fortunata Viti
- Michael the Archangel
- Syncletica

Toothaches
- Apollonia
- Christopher
- Elizabeth of Hungary
- Ida of Nivelles
- Kea
- Medard
- Osmund

Traveling, finding lodging
- Gertrude of Nivelles
- Julian the Hospitaller

Unborn children
- Gerard Majella
- Joseph

Understanding
- Holy Spirit

Unemployed people
- Cajetan

Universal Church
- Joseph
- Peter the Apostle

Unmarried girls
- Andrew the Apostle
- Catherine of Alexandria
- Nicholas of Myra

Vanity
- Rose of Lima

Veterinarians; animal doctors
- Blaise
- Eligius
- James the Greater

Virgins
- Agnes of Rome
- Blessed Virgin Mary

Virtue
- Hallvard

Vocations
- Alphonsus Maria de Liguori

- Infant Jesus of Prague

Women
- Margaret of Antioch
- Mary Magalen

Women who wish to become mothers
- Andrew the Apostle

Women whose husbands are at war
- Daniel of Padua

World Youth Day
- Adolph Kolping
- Albertus Magnus
- Balthasar
- Boniface
- Caspar
- Melchior
- Teresa Benedicta of the Cross
- Ursula

Young people
- Aloysius Gonzaga
- Gabriel of the Sorrowful
- Stanislaus Kostka
- Teresa of the Andes
- Valentine

Zoos
- Francis of Assisi

CALENDAR OF FEAST DAYS

Feast Days in January

1. Mary, Mother of God
2. St. Basil the Great
3. Most Holy Name of Jesus
4. St. Elizabeth Ann Seton
5. St. John Neumann
6. St. Gregory Nazianzen
7. St. Raymond of Penyafort
8. Blessed Angela of Foligno
9. St. Adrian of Canterbury
10. St. Gregory of Nyssa
11. Blessed William Carter
12. St. Marguerite Bourgeoys
13. St. Hilary
14. Servant of God John the Gardener
15. St. Paul the Hermit
16. St. Berard and Companions
17. St. Anthony of Egypt
18. St. Charles of Sezze
19. St. Fabian
20. St. Sebastian
21. St. Agnes
22. St. Vincent
23. Blessed Mother Marianne Cope
24. St. Francis de Sales
25. Conversion of St. Paul
26. Sts. Timothy and Titus
27. St. Angela Merici
28. St. Thomas Aquinas
29. Servant of God Brother Juniper
30. St. Hyacintha of Mariscotti
31. St. John Bosco

Feast Days in February

1. St. Ansgar
2. Presentation of the Lord
3. St. Blase
4. St. Joseph of Leonissa
5. St. Agatha
6. St. Paul Miki and Companions
7. St. Colette
8. St. Josephine Bakhita

9. St. Jerome Emiliani
10. St. Scholastica
11. Our Lady of Lourdes
12. St. Apollonia
13. St. Giles Mary
of St. Joseph
14. Sts. Cyril and Methodius
15. St. Claude la
Colombière
16. St. Gilbert of
Sempringham
17. Seven Founders of the
Order of Servites
18. Blessed John of Fiesole
19. St. Conrad of Piacenza
20. Blessed Jacinta and
Francisco Marto
21. St. Peter Damian
22. Chair of Peter
the Apostle
23. St. Polycarp
24. Blessed Luke Belludi
25. Blessed Sebastian
of Aparicio
26. St. Porphyry of Gaza
27. St. Gabriel of Our
Lady of Sorrows
28. Blessed Daniel Brottier

Feast Days in March

1. St. David of Wales
2. St. Agnes of Bohemia
3. St. Katharine Drexel
4. St. Casimir
5. St. John Joseph
of the Cross
6. Servant of God
Sylvester of Assisi
7. Sts. Perpetua
and Felicity

8. St. John of God
9. St. Frances of Rome
10. St. Dominic Savio
11. St. John Ogilvie
12. Blessed Angela Salawa
13. St. Leander of Seville
14. St. Maximilian
15. St. Louise de Marillac
16. St. Clement Mary
Hofbauer
17. St. Patrick
18. St. Cyril of Jerusalem
19. St. Joseph
20. St. Salvator of Horta
21. Blessed John of Parma
22. St. Nicholas Owen
23. St. Turibius of
Mogrovejo
24. St. Catherine of Genoa
25. Annunciation
of the Lord
26. Blessed Didacus
of Cadiz
27. Blessed Francis
Faà di Bruno
28. St. Hesychius of
Jerusalem
29. Blessed Ludovico
of Casoria
30. St. Peter Regalado
31. St. Stephen of Mar Saba

Feast Days in April

1. St. Hugh of Grenoble
2. St. Francis of Paola
3. St. Benedict the African
4. St. Isidore of Seville
5. St. Vincent Ferrer
6. St. Crescentia Hoess

7. St. John Baptist
   de la Salle
8. St. Julie Billiart
9. St. Casilda
10. St. Magdalen of Canossa
11. St. Stanislaus
12. St. Teresa of Los Andes
13. St. Martin I
14. Blessed Peter Gonzalez
15. Blessed Caesar de Bus
16. St. Bernadette Soubirous
17. St. Benedict
    Joseph Labre
18. Blessed James Oldo
19. Blessed Luchesio
    and Buonadonna
20. St. Conrad of Parzham
21. St. Anselm
22. St. Adalbert of Prague
23. St. George
24. St. Fidelis of
    Sigmaringen
25. St. Mark
26. St. Pedro de San
    José Betancur
27. St. Louis Mary
    de Montfort
28. St. Peter Chanel
29. St. Catherine of Siena
30. St. Pius V

Feast Days in May

1. St. Joseph the Worker
2. St. Athanasius
3. Sts. Philip and James
4. Blessed Michael
   Giedroyc
5. St. Hilary of Arles
6. Sts. Marian and James
7. Blessed Rose Venerini

8. St. Peter of Tarentaise
9. St. Catharine of Bologna
10. Blessed Damien
    of Molokai
11. St. Ignatius of Laconi
12. Sts. Nereus and
    Achilleus
13. Our Lady of Fatima
14. St. Matthias
15. St. Isidore the Farmer
16. St. Margaret of Cortona
17. St. Paschal Baylon
18. St. John I
19. St. Theophilus of Corte
20. St. Bernardine of Siena
21. St. Cristóbal Magallanes
    and Companions
22. St. Rita of Cascia
23. St. Felix of Cantalice
24. St. Mary Magdalene
    de Pazzi
25. St. Bede the Venerable
26. St. Philip Neri
27. St. Augustine of
    Canterbury
28. St. Mary Ann of
    Jesus of Paredes
29. St. Madeleine
    Sophie Barat
30. St. Gregory VII
31. Visitation

Feast Days in June

1. St. Justin
2. Sts. Marcellinus
   and Peter
3. Blessed John XXIII
4. Charles Lwanga
   & Companions
5. St. Boniface

6. St. Norbert
7. Servant of God
   Joseph Perez
8. St. William of York
9. St. Ephrem
10. Blessed Joachima
11. St. Barnabas
12. Blessed Jolenta
    (Yolanda) of Poland
13. St. Anthony of Padua
14. St. Albert Chmielowski
15. Servant of God
    Orlando Catanii
16. St. John Francis Regis
17. St. Joseph Cafasso
18. Venerable Matt Talbot
19. St. Romuald
20. St. Paulinus of Nola
21. St. Aloysius Gonzaga
22. St. Thomas More
23. St. John Fisher
24. Birth of John the Baptist
25. Blessed Jutta of
    Thuringia
26. Blessed Raymond Lull
27. St. Cyril of Alexandria
28. St. Irenaeus
29. Sts. Peter and Paul
30. First Martyrs of the
    Church of Rome

Feast Days in July

1. Blessed Junipero Serra
2. St. Oliver Plunkett
3. St. Thomas the Apostle
4. St. Elizabeth of Portugal
5. St. Anthony Zaccaria
6. St. Maria Goretti
7. Blessed Emmanuel
   Ruiz & Companions

8. St. Gregory Grassi
   & Companions
9. St. Augustine Zhao
   Rong & Companions
10. St. Veronica Giuliani
11. St. Benedict
12. Sts. John Jones
    and John Wall
13. St. Henry
14. Blessed Kateri
    Tekakwitha
15. St. Bonaventure
16. Our Lady of
    Mount Carmel
17. St. Francis Solano
18. Blessed Angeline
    of Marsciano
19. Servant of God Francis
    Garces & Companions
20. St. Apollinaris
21. St. Lawrence of Brindisi
22. St. Mary Magdalene
23. St. Bridget
24. St. Sharbel Makhlouf
25. St. James the Greater
26. Sts. Joachim and Ann
27. Blessed Antonio Lucci
28. St. Leopold Mandic
29. St. Martha
30. St. Peter Chrysologus
31. St. Ignatius of Loyola

Feast Days in August

1. St. Alphonsus Liguori
2. St. Eusebius of Vercelli
3. St. Peter Julian Eymard
4. St. John Vianney
5. Dedication of St.
   Mary Major Basilica

6. Transfiguration of the Lord
7. St. Cajetan
8. St. Dominic
9. St. Teresa Benedicta of the Cross (Edith Stein)
10. St. Lawrence
11. St. Clare
12. St. Louis of Toulouse
13. Sts. Pontian and Hippolytus
14. St. Maximilian Mary Kolbe
15. Assumption of Mary
16. St. Stephen of Hungary
17. St. Joan of the Cross
18. St. Jane Frances de Chantal
19. St. John Eudes
20. St. Bernard of Clairvaux
21. St. Pius X
22. Queenship of Mary
23. St. Rose of Lima
24. St. Bartholomew
25. St. Louis of France
26. St. Joseph Calasanz
27. St. Monica
28. St. Augustine
29. Beheading of John the Baptist
30. Blessed Jeanne Jugan
31. Sts. Joseph of Arimathea & Nicodemus

Feast Days in September

1. St. Giles
2. Blessed John Francis Burté & Companions
3. St. Gregory the Great
4. St. Rose of Viterbo
5. Blessed Mother Teresa of Calcutta
6. Blessed Claudio Granzotto
7. Blessed Frederick Ozanam
8. Birth of Mary
9. St. Peter Claver
10. St. Thomas of Villanova
11. St. Cyprian
12. Holy Name of Mary
13. St. John Chrysostom
14. Triumph of the Cross
15. Our Lady of Sorrows
16. St. Cornelius
17. St. Robert Bellarmine
18. St. Joseph of Cupertino
19. St. Januarius
20. Andrew Kim Taegon, Paul
21. Chong Hasang & Companions
22. St. Matthew
23. St. Lawrence Ruiz & Companions
24. St. Padre Pio da Pietrelcina
25. St. Pacifico of San Severino
26. St. Elzear & Blessed Delphina
27. Sts. Cosmas & Damian

28. St. Vincent de Paul
29. St. Wenceslaus
30. Michael, Gabriel
    & Raphael
31. St. Jerome

Feast Days in October

1. St. Thérèse of Lisieux
2. Feast of the
   Guardian Angels
3. Blessed Francis
   Xavier Seelos
4. St. Francis of Assisi
5. St. Faustina
6. St. Bruno
7. Our Lady of the Rosary
8. St. John Leonardi
9. St. Denis & Companions
10. St. Francis Borgia
11. Blessed Angela
    Truszkowska
12. St. Seraphin of
    Montegranaro
13. St. Margaret Mary
    Alacoque
14. St. Callistus I
15. St. Teresa of Avila
16. St. Marguerite d'Youville
17. St. Ignatius of Antioch
18. St. Luke
19. St. Isaac Jogues, John de
    Brébeuf & Companions
20. St. Maria Bertilla
    Boscardin
21. St. Hilarion
22. St. Peter of Alcantara
23. St. John of Capistrano
24. St. Anthony Claret

25. Blessed Antônio de
    Sant'Anna Galvão
26. Blessed Contardo Ferrini
27. Blessed Bartholomew
    of Vicenza
28. Sts. Simon & Jude
29. St. Narcissus of
    Jerusalem
30. St. Alphonsus Rodriguez
31. St. Wolfgang of
    Regensburg

Feast Days in November

1. Feast of All Saints
2. Feast of All Souls
3. St. Martin de Porres
4. St. Charles Borromeo
5. Venerable
   Solanus Casey
6. St. Nicholas Tavelic
   & Companions
7. St. Didacus
8. Blessed John
   Duns Scotus
9. Dedication of St.
   John Lateran
10. St. Leo the Great
11. St. Martin of Tours
12. St. Josaphat
13. St. Frances Xavier
    Cabrini
14. St. Gertrude
15. St. Albert the Great
16. St. Margaret of Scotland
17. St. Elizabeth of Hungary
18. Dedication of St.
    Peter & Paul
19. St. Agnes of Assisi

20. St. Rose Philippine Duchesne
21. Feast of the Presentation of Mary
22. St. Cecilia
23. Blessed Miguel Agustín Pro
24. St. Andrew Dung-Lac & Companions
25. St. Columban
26. St. Catherine of Alexandria
27. St. Francesco Antonio Fasani
28. St. James of the Marche
29. Servant of God John of Monte Corvino
30. St. Andrew

16. Blessed Honoratus Kozminski
17. Lazarus
18. Blessed Anthony Grassi
19. Blessed Pope Urban V
20. St. Dominic of Silos
21. St. Peter Canisius
22. Blessed Jacopone da Todi
23. St. John of Kanty
24. Christmas at Greccio
25. Christmas Day
26. St. Stephen
27. St. John the Apostle
28. Feast of the Holy Innocents
29. St. Thomas Becket
30. St. Egwin
31. St. Sylvester I

Feast Days in December

1. Blessed John of Vercelli
2. Blessed Rafal Chylinski
3. St. Francis Xavier
4. St. John Damascene
5. St. Sabas
6. St. Nicholas
7. St. Ambrose
8. Feast of the Immaculate Conception
9. St. Juan Diego
10. Blessed Adolph Kolping
11. St. Damasus I
12. Our Lady of Guadalupe
13. St. Lucy
14. St. John of the Cross
15. Blessed Mary Frances Schervier